Questioning Education

In the post-pandemic world, how can we rethink the future of education as a system, process, and tradition to make lasting changes? This thought-provoking book by Sean Slade reminds us that education prepares students for their futures and yet has become stuck in the past. Slade asks us to move from our focus on education as a content-delivery system and instead reflect on its overarching purpose(s). He shows how we can shift our systems and our curriculum discussions away from beginning with the *What* and *How*, and instead start with the *Why* and *Who*.

Utilizing the metaphor of an educational solar system, he explains how fundamental questions we ask ourselves influence subsequent actions and subsequent questions. The book outlines how this is different from current trends such as PBL and service learning, how it can work in the content areas, how it can make learning relevant and meaningful, and even how it can improve tolerance and community. Throughout the book, Slade dares us to not just ponder these topics but to take the first step of real action.

Whether you're a teacher or a leader, you will be inspired to reconsider what school is and what you have the power to do about it, so we can all play a role in improving ourselves, our systems, and our world.

Sean Slade is a global education leader with more than 25 years of experience in education globally, in a career spanning four continents and five countries. Currently residing in the Washington DC area, he has driven policy change, implemented initiatives, and developed educational leaders to enhance the social impact of education.

T0383446

Questioning Education

Moving from What and How to Why and Who

Sean Slade

Routledge
Taylor & Francis Group

NEW YORK AND LONDON

First published 2022
by Routledge
605 Third Avenue, New York, NY 10158

and by Routledge
4 Park Square, Milton Park, Abingdon, Oxon, OX14 4RN

Routledge is an imprint of the Taylor & Francis Group, an informa business

Library of Congress Cataloging-in-Publication Data
A catalog record for this title has been requested

ISBN: 978-1-032-13191-7 (hbk)
ISBN: 978-1-032-11741-6 (pbk)
ISBN: 978-1-003-22806-6 (ebk)

DOI: 10.4324/9781003228066

Typeset in Palatino
by Newgen Publishing UK

To Peter and Caitlin, and curious children everywhere.

Contents

Meet the Author

Sean Slade is a global education leader, speaker, and author, with nearly three decades of experience in education, who resides in the Washington DC area. With a strong background in education reform and wellbeing, he has driven policy change, implemented initiatives, and developed educational leaders to enhance the social impact of education. He has helped lead the whole child movement in education, focusing on a  more learner-centered and holistic approach to education, and has been a leading advocate for the alignment of health and education. A former teacher, head of department, and educational researcher, he currently serves as the Head of Education at BTS Spark, North America, a not-for-profit practice focusing on developing the next generation of school leaders. He is a Social & Emotional Learning expert for NBC Today, advisory member for the OECD's Future of Education & Skills 2030, and a founding member of the UNESCO Chair on Global Health & Education, and has written for the *Washington Post*, *Huffington Post*, *EdWeek*, and been published by ASCD, Abingdon Press, Human Kinetics, and Routledge.

"Three and two make five. Five and seven, twelve. Twelve and three, fifteen. Fifteen and seven, twenty-two. Twenty-two and six, twenty-eight. No time to light it again. Twenty-six and five, thirty-one. Whew! That amounts to five-hundred-and-one million, six-hundred-twenty-two thousand, seven hundred thirty-one."

"Five-hundred million what?."

"Hmm? You're still there? Five-hundred-and-one million... I don't remember ... I have so much work to do! I'm a serious man. I can't be bothered with trifles! Two and five, seven..."

"Five-hundred-and-one million what?" Repeated the little prince, who had never in his life let go of a question once he has asked it.

The Little Prince (1943)[1]

In 1943, Antoine de Saint-Exupéry raised a series of fundamental questions asking us both about our world and about who we are, via his protagonist the Little Prince. This book seeks to do the same but using the frame of our education systems, which it should be noted are there for the purpose of helping us discover more about our world and ourselves.

Note

1   Saint-Exupéry, A. & Woods, K., *The Little Prince*, 1943. Print.

Preface

This is not the first book to question education nor will it, nor should it, ever be the last. It must consistently be questioned. Education is the system and sector that literally prepares our youth for the future and must be constantly changing itself to suit new and upcoming needs, contexts, and outcomes. Education both prepares us for the new world and helps prepare that new world for us.

This book rests on the work of others, and in recent years this includes the work and thinking of Yong Zhao, Ross Hall, Andy Hargreaves, Dennis Shirley, and Pasi Sahlberg. It rests on the wise words and questions of the late Rita Pierson, and the push towards a growth mindset of Angela Duckworth. It aligns with the thinking of Valerie Hannon and the desire to have our youth thrive.

But more than others it rests on the work and paths created by Simon Sinek and the late Sir Ken Robinson. Sir Ken reframed the debate around education's purpose to place creativity at the core and to task us with discarding the industrial frame of education that too many systems still utilize. Simon, though talking from a business perspective, placed the reason – the *why* – at the center and asked us all to rethink what we do based around this fundamental question.

This book takes the core of both these works to re-ask what our education system is for. It asks us to question education itself in order to improve ourselves, our systems, and our world.

Introduction

Annus Horribilis and a Time for Change

This year 2020–2021, unlike any other, has made us rethink what we do. It's given us time to reflect and question everything. From where we go, to who we see. From what we prioritize, to what we are or are not prepared to risk. While much of this has been a literal exploration of survival, it has also provided us the opportunity – also unlike any other – to reconsider what we do and ask ourselves why we do it. Education as a system, as a process, and as a tradition, is not immune from this introspection.

> Education as a system, as a process, and as a tradition, is not immune from this introspection.

We have seen states discard the holy grail of test taking. We have watched as compliance has given way to compassion, and we have been equally engaged and bemused of the talk of getting back to normal. In truth the only thing most of us are seeking is more a return to that feeling of 'normalcy' rather than a return to a system and a process that has been, for far too long, inadequate, inequitable, and antiquated.

This *annus horribilis* has given us a unique chance to appraise what we do in education and potentially propel it into the future. If there was ever a sector, or an industry, that should be at the cutting

DOI: 10.4324/9781003228066-1

edge of innovation, it is education, whose whole raison d'etre is preparing those soon to be living in the future for the future. Yet education for too long has appeared less the sails of a ship pushing it forward to new horizons and more of the anchor stuck to a sea floor and restricting its own progress. 2020 and 2021, it seems, has compelled us to raise the anchor from the rocks and we are starting to discuss where we want to go. Sure, the spinnaker hasn't yet been cast but the crew are at least talking.

We are questioning education as a profession and as a society. This has started off benignly enough with debates over remote versus in-person teaching and learning, and discussion over the merits and flaws of both. It has allowed (or forced) students to develop more agency in their own learning and required teachers to become more of that 'guide on the side' that so many in education circles have been demanding for over a decade. It has begun a questioning around our processes and practices which, to be honest, couldn't come soon enough.

These are not questions that have appeared out of nowhere – these are questions that are being asked and have been asked in the education sector for a while now. The difference now is that it is not just a progressive school in upstate New York or an innovative district in Washington state asking this. These discussions are percolating into everyday conversation across social media and into family dinner chats. These topics, perhaps buoyed by the forced parental involvement of at-home, online learning, are entering the general public consciousness more than before, with discussion about the processes of education from its daily methods to its intended outcomes.

The closest we have come to this point in garnering the public's attention and imagination around what education could and should be was the widely popular and compelling Sir Ken Robinson TED talk, 'Do Schools Kill Creativity?' – still one of the most viewed TED talks ever and yet still unfortunately as relevant in 2021 as it was in 2006. That in itself should illustrate the intransigence of the education sector. That the great insights of Sir Ken have also been lost to us in 2020[1] is another mark of a tragic year.

I believe our only hope for the future is to adopt a new concept of human ecology, one in which we start to reconstitute our conception of the richness of human capacity. Our education system has mined our minds in the way we strip-mined the earth for a particular commodity. We have to rethink the fundamental principles in which we are educating our children.

Robinson (2006)[2]

But we do now have the attention of the public – the teachers, principals, policymakers, and even parents. We even have, though quicky waning via never-ending Zoom lessons, the attention of the students themselves. And, therefore, it is time to act.

My call here is not to have us tinker at the unit plan or to recraft the curriculum to make it more conducive to online asynchronous learning but to question education itself. Start with the end in mind and plan backwards. What is it that we want education to do? What is its purpose?

Purpose of Education

This isn't a new question, truth be told. It has been asked, and asked often, but too often only answered by those in discrete circles. The debate has circled the halls of education faculty and sometimes entered into teacher preparation courses. But it has rarely been discussed in school buildings, nor at Parent-Teacher Association meetings, nor by students themselves. It has, at best, been a discussion of mission and philosophy that has remained at the mission statement level of school and district policy in terms of outcomes and impact. And even if it has been articulated in the mission statement it has rarely filtered down into the classroom, across the curriculum, or had much impact on the learning of students themselves.

> What is the purpose of education? This question agitates scholars, teachers, statesmen, every group, in fact, of thoughtful men and women. The conventional answer is the acquisition of knowledge, the reading of books, and the learning of facts. Perhaps because there are so many books and the branches of knowledge in which we can learn facts are so multitudinous today, we begin to hear more frequently that the function of education is to give children a desire to learn and to teach them how to use their minds and where to go to acquire facts when their curiosity is aroused. Even more all-embracing than this is the statement made not long ago, before a group of English headmasters, by the Archbishop of York, that "the true purpose of education is to produce citizens."
>
> Roosevelt (1930)[3]

> The purpose of education has always been to every one, in essence, the same—to give the young, the things they need in order to develop in an orderly, sequential way into members of society.
>
> Dewey (1934)[4]

[E]ducation has a two-fold function to perform in the life of man and in society: the one is utility and the other is culture. Education must enable a man to become more efficient, to achieve with increasing facility the legitimate goals of his life.

Luther King Jr. (1947)[5]

Notes

1   Bates, S., 'Sir Ken Robinson Obituary', *The Guardian*, August 26, 2020.
2   Robinson, K., 'Do Schools Kill Creativity?," *TED2006* talk, 2006.
3   Roosevelt, E., 'Good Citizenship: The Purpose of Education,' *Pictorial Review*, April 1930, archived in *Yearbook of the National Society for the Study of Education*, October 2008.
4   Dewey, J., 'Individual Psychology and Education,' *The Philosopher*, Vol. XII (1934).
5   King, M.L. Jr., 'The Purpose of Education,' *Maroon Tiger*, January–February 1947.

Part 1

The Educational Solar System

1

Changing the Educational Solar System

Why have we not been able to prise away this discussion on the purpose of education from the philosophers to the practitioners? Why have we not been able to empower the learners and the teachers themselves in this necessary dialogue?

We have left the discussion of purpose to those who have succeeded out of a system that has benefited them but alienated others. We should be raising the fundamental questions of purpose with and across those who are not fitting in with the current system as much as we do with those for whom it has been constructed.

And my premise – and it is just a premise – is that we have been asking the wrong questions of education's purpose from the start. Or at least the purpose of education needs to change from teaching us *what* we should know to *why* we should know it.

> . . . the purpose of education needs to change from teaching us *what* we should know to *why* we should know it.

It is a change in our educational ecosystem, or to put it another way, in our educational solar system. No longer should we orbit the *What* and

> No longer should we orbit the *What* and secondarily the *How* in what is learned. But rather we should be focused primarily on the *Why* followed by the *Who*.

DOI: 10.4324/9781003228066-3

secondarily the *How* in what is learned. But rather we should be focused primarily on the *Why* followed by the *Who*.

Status Quo

If we placed these interrogative words, or fundamental questions, that are directing education itself into a hierarchy they would currently look something like this, with the first having more influence and authority than the next. We determine what should be learned first and then we worry about its context, meaning, value to the learner, and finally its purpose later – often as a mere afterthought.

◆ What
◆ How
◆ When
◆ Where
◆ Who
◆ Why

The *What* dominates and is followed closely by *How*. How a *What* is learned to be precise but *How* also in terms of learning a skill or a trade. *Who* we are and *Why* something is learned are too often relegated to the periphery or worse still never asked or considered.

> We have lived and learned via a system that places *What* at the center.

We have lived and learned via a system that places *What* at the center. *What* has been the dominant force, the dominant star in our educational solar system, with all other planets revolving around and responsive to that question. Just as in our own solar system there is dominance and influence that comes with being core. Other movements, other questions, become subsidiary and at most responsive to the core. This has meant that *How* relates to *What*. *How* in this relationship is less about how to learn and more about learning how to do something – a skill, a task, a function. *How* only has relevance due to its relationship, and close relationship, to what has been determined is necessary to be learned.

And what of the remaining questions – *Where, When,* and lastly *Who* and *Why*. Depending upon the school and its teachers, they play less and less of a role the further they are from the central question.

Where and *When* provide context but only in relation to *What* is being learned and not in relation to *Who* is learning or *Why* they are learning. The base of this relationship still emanates from the content and the learner remains secondary. Content may be adjusted by skilled teachers, but the content is still king, and it is still up to the learner to adapt themselves to the content rather than the other way around. And the *Why* – the purpose of learning – is likely never discussed, debated, discerned, or accounted for.

To extend the educational solar system metaphor we can place these questions as a set of planets orbiting at different rates, and at varying distance, from the center. Each one revolves around the center but is also influenced by those closer to it. Depending on the school and its teachers, the degree of influence one planet has over another or the proximity it holds may change, but the foundations remain the same – *What* at the core and *Why* off into the far reaches of space.

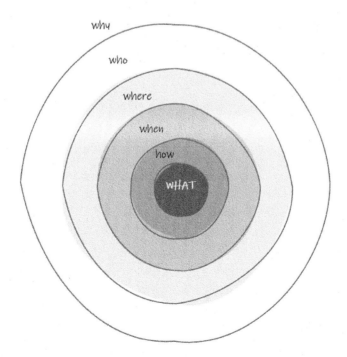

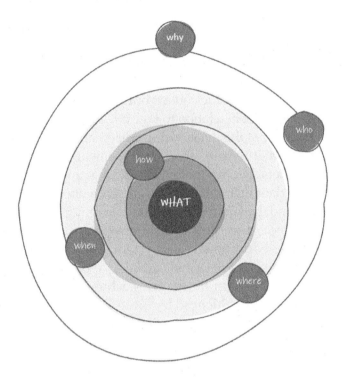

A New Educational Solar System

But how would this look if we began, as we always should, with *Why*? What would happen if we flipped this solar system? *Why* starts to answer the purpose and the purpose must be related to the learner (*Who*). Imagine for a moment an educational system that was dominated by *Why* and *Who*. Each learner, each community, is questioning and responding to learning based on its purpose and its meaning – and at the same time its meaning as it relates to them and their community. Such an educational solar system would look something like this.

- ◆ Why
- ◆ Who
- ◆ Where
- ◆ When
- ◆ How
- ◆ What

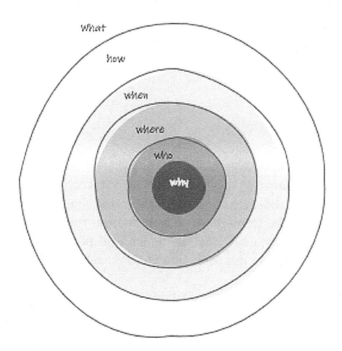

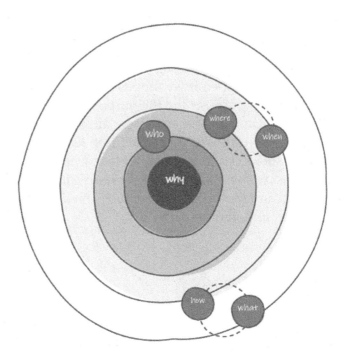

But perhaps more so, rather than just a hierarchy, as planets themselves interact and influence they would be arrayed as sets, or groups, that exert combined influence, with *Why* at the core.

- ◆ Why
- ◆ Who
- ◆ Where and When
- ◆ How and What

Who becomes a leading question for each individual to discover who they are and who they may become. *Who* also encapsulates the immediate 'I' but also the future 'I.' *Who* am I? *Who* will I become? *Who* at the same time incorporates the individual but also the collective we. *Who* are we? *Who* will we become?

These are fundamental questions that to my thinking encapsulate a key function of education – understanding the many *Why*'s of the world and understanding ourselves. Their fundamental need and influence should therefore impact and draw in the remaining questions. *What* and *How* are not dismissed nor ignored but instead related to the core questions of *Why* and *Who*. The starting point

> The starting point becomes the purpose and the learner, while the content and the skills become responsive to them.

becomes the purpose and the learner, while the content and the skills become responsive to them.

Where and *When* take on new influence as they relate again to the learner and not the content.

The placement of all of these secondary questions or planets is debatable. Should *Where* and *When* have greater influence over *What* and *How* – likely yes. Should *What* and *How* be responsive to *Where* and *When*? Should *When* have greater impact than *Where*? – maybe. All these relationships are fluid and their impact (rate of revolutions, peripheral distance) and even their impact on each other is connected.

The key here is placing the fundamental questions – *Why* and then *Who* – at the core and arraying the remaining key questions around that foundation.

This does not dismiss the need for *What* is being learned nor *How* it should be best performed but rather puts them into context. In order for something to be learned it should have a reason – a reason connected to the person, their community, their world, and their place in it.

> In order for something to be learned it should have a reason – a reason connected to the person, their community, their world, and their place in it.

2

A Journey Through the New Educational Solar System

Why

We have spent decades, or perhaps centuries, telling children and youth what we believe they need to know. We have spent thousands of hours pushing facts, dates, formula, which we are told – and we tell the students – are necessary requirements to enter society, the workforce, or to undertake further study. But at the very same time we often have been unable to answer one of the simplest of questions asked everyday in a multitude of classrooms: 'why do we need to learn this?'

> We load the subjects and then we load the students' schedules and their proverbial backpacks, to see how much they can carry.

As the amount of information increases exponentially annually, subjects have become ladened-down content packhorses that compete in acts of absurd strength and endurance to see which can carry the largest load. We load the subjects and then we load the students' schedules and their proverbial backpacks, to see how much they can carry.

DOI: 10.4324/9781003228066-4

And then we lament the increasing pandemics of anxiety, stress, disengagement, and declining youth wellbeing. We shout into this storm of increasing content and pressure that children should try to relax, go outside, play and have fun, enjoy their youth, while at the very same time increasing their burdens.

Well-meaning teachers struggle to find relevance, meaning, and context for their students, all the while knowing that much of what is being taught is peripheral at best and often merely a grading pit-stop in our educational rat-race. We have the right intentions but we're in the wrong pursuit.

Yet we know that children are curious. We know that learners seek answers to things they, or we, don't understand or want to understand better. We lament that young children start off curious and then, soon into elementary school, and definitely by middle school, their curiosity has been wiped. They have learned to not ask why, or if they do, they will receive a curt response.

We actively silence curiosity in our younger students and then absurdly hold it open to those who have mastered the K12, or rather P20, education system. Debate, discussion, and divergent views are held up as gold medals for those who have successfully endured primary and secondary education. Once someone has entered university, or sometimes after they have received their degree, they can now be allowed to be philosophers, ideators, and creators.

The more logical place to start is however not with *What* but with *Why*. If we began structuring education around our innate curiosity and not primarily around content or even skills, our system would develop rationale and inherent meaning.

> If we began structuring education around our innate curiosity and not primarily around content or even skills, our system would develop rationale and inherent meaning.

But what would an education system based around *Why* look like? Varied, different, but very targeted and personalized.

At its core we could assume that it would be as simple as never having a student having to ask 'why are we learning this?,' but really it's much more likely to mean that the question is rather always asked. The major difference would be that the question is now always respected, answered, and discussed.

Playing this scenario through, it would also mean that education becomes much more personalized, focusing on what the class, context, and student, in discussion with the teacher, deems most meaningful.

This in turn means that the teacher would have to be much more autonomous, with greater control and agency over what is taught and how it is introduced. It would not make learning devoid of content or skills but rather it would array these around meaning and purpose, and this meaning and purpose would be owned by each learner in the context of their settings.

The teacher would be less the deliverer of content and more so the pedagogical expert, helping determine value and meaning through conversations with students, and then structuring learning journeys in discussion with the students, their peers, and their community.

Ultimately, standards and benchmarks, along with assessments, would change as they would need to be focused around mastery of understanding and exhibiting how knowledge across a variety of areas has been achieved. The learning would need to show relevance and it would need to demonstrate growth.

At the same time, it would at its core change what teachers teach, and would require them to question and discuss the relevance of anything teachable. This may, or may not, change fundamentally what is being taught but would change fundamentally why it is being taught. Literature, poetry, and journalism would likely still be part of a system but the rationale for them may shift to be more focused on developing empathy; understanding others; explaining emotions and reactions; absorbing alternative viewpoints. Economics, Civics, and History all continue to play roles in increasing our understanding of our communities, societies, and world, and in doing so would likely continue to expand both our curiosity and help answer our questions. Math would likely be core, but core to solving solutions. Physical activity and education would be adjusted to encourage lifelong activity, well-being, increasing our own personal development and connection local to the community. To some the change could be minimal; to others it would be dramatic. To everyone it has the potential to be freeing and purposeful.

A system based on *Why* would logically then develop a generation of learners who question, debate, push back, dialogue, seek solutions, and assume agency. These are the skills, attributes, and competencies that both society and industry are seeking. A system based on *Why* would additionally help grow and develop transformative competencies, including creating new value; reconciling tensions and dilemmas; and taking responsibility (OECD, 2018).[1]

> A system based on *Why* would logically then develop a generation of learners who question, debate, push back, dialogue, seek solutions, and assume agency.

Focusing on *Why* would mean a readjustment to our school days and our scheduling. It would mean an alteration and reappraisal of what is assessed and change how learning should be assessed. It would mean a change to a system of education that has served to produce workers and personnel who are not encouraged to question. But our world has changed, and is changing. Our world needs solutions to new questions, and needs generations of learners who are apt to question, debate nuance, and ask why.

> Our world needs solutions to new questions, and needs generations of learners who are apt to question, debate nuance, and ask why.

Who

But for *Why* to have relevance it must be aligned or attached to the person doing the learning – the learner. So, *Who* is this learner? *Who* are they now? *Who* do they hope to become? *Who* are we and *Who* do we want to become?

That surely is a premise for an education system, allowing or perhaps creating the scenarios where individuals discover more about themselves, what they are skilled at, what they are passionate about, what they didn't or wouldn't discover about themselves unless a learning situation was developed to help them discover that.

Personalized learning, project-based learning, and individual education plans all move in this direction of putting the learner nearer the center and organizing the learning to take place around that individual. Via personalization the content still mirrors the standard curriculum and stems from a basis of *What* but at least it has been modified to allow for individual perspectives, strengths, weaknesses, and some degree of voice. It is a step in the right direction but it has originated – as with the majority of our teaching – from a beginning of *What*.

> The true lessons learned through a drama or musical performance may not be the music or acting themselves but the ability to push oneself and do more than the learner expected.

Subject areas that align better to the *Who* in our current system are the Arts. Drama, Music, and Fine Arts allow the learner to discover via their settings and mediums to discover more about themselves. They allow people to learn about who they are and what – in relatively safe settings – they can become, conquer, or master. The true lessons learned through a drama or musical performance may not be the music or acting themselves but the ability to push oneself and do more than the learner expected.

By practicing and performing, the learner discovers that they are perhaps capable of facing their fears, or they discover a passion for being in front of others that without the stage they wouldn't have discovered.

They may also discover they dislike this environment and are therefore allowed to make a conscious decision to move away from that setting.

The problem currently though is that these subject areas are few and far between. If you don't discover yourself in Drama or Music, then there is less chance that you can discover yourself in Algebra 2. It's not impossible nor inconceivable, but the structure of such subjects is not based around self-discovery.

But imagine for a moment if every subject area – if we even maintain them as structures – allowed the learner to explore and experiment. Imagine if the same degree of flexibility and voice was incorporated into Literature or Math or Physics as it is in the Arts. Discovery would not have to come at the expense of putting yourself literally on stage but by solving problems that have relevance and meaning to the learner.

Imagine one step further where journeys or learning units are created that purposefully plan out self-discovery or purposefully plan out experiences that extend or enhance one's self-efficacy. These learning activities and environments are happening in our schools but too often they are sidelined as options or added into traditional forms of teaching and learning. But research shows the great benefits of project-based learning,[2] inquiry-based learning,[3] exploratory and discovery-based learning,[4] or even expeditionary learning.[5] These benefits extend beyond the academic and influence the development of the whole person – their self-efficacy, their self-belief, their empathy for others, as well as their problem solving and collaboration skills. Research by the famed John Hattie[6] early in his career also highlighted the civic benefits that arise from engagement in exploratory learning – in particular Outward Bound – and learners' changing attitude towards civic responsibility and engagement.

Who are you also quickly becomes *who* are we? *Who* are we as a community of learners? *Who* are we as a community? *Who* are we as a society? And this, in itself, places more onus on the question of why. *Why* does our society do what it does and is this what we want our future society to look like? It does not necessarily alter our communities or societies but it does put them up for questioning and rationalization. To a certain extent we do this already, and some educators and schools more than others. Service learning, community service, and student councils all play into this realm and ask or allow students to ask questions to learn about their surroundings and environments. They dabble in providing a local or global context to questions and issues, sparking interest in some but too often presented in isolation apart from other content learned in other subject areas.

But imagine for a moment a year of learning about who you are, who we are, and who you/we could become. Imagine the common thread passed through books read, play enacted, visits taken, history learned that allowed you to discover yourself. Interspersed with current affairs, current trends, and current dilemmas. Some may already be doing this work, albeit as an adjunct to the necessary curriculum and benchmarks. Some may have already understood this to be their calling in teaching – allowing each child to learn more about themselves and their potential. And the fact that some are already doing this shows to the rest of us that this is both possible and achievable now. What must change first is not the structures but the mindsets. Change our fundamental questions of education and we change why we value it and what it can achieve.

> What must change first is not the structures but the mindsets. Change our fundamental questions of education and we change why we value it and what it can achieve.

Where and When

Where and *When* places the learning in context. It provides a frame for *Why* something is relevant or to *Who* it may be meaningful. Place and time. Culture and context. Relevance and meaning.

We have been adjusting our learning to culture and context, place and time for a while; however, this has come out of the discussion around content and skills. *What* and *How* has required us to adjust to suit the level and understanding of the learner.

What this flipped educational solar system does is change the paradigm so that the relevance of time and place comes from the context of *Why* we are learning something and *Who* is learning. Out of this the content and the skills can then be determined.

> What this flipped educational solar system does is change the paradigm so that the relevance of time and place comes from the context of *Why* we are learning something and *Who* is learning.

Where signifies locational context and cultural context. This could be a school community, a larger community, or a regional, national or global community.

When, however, frames timespans and asks what is current or relevant from a historical and current context. What is occurring currently? *How* is this related to what has occurred previously? Why is this relevant now and *how* can this help explain things in the future? *How* can this help build additional meaning? Aligned with *Where* it provides a fuller frame for meaning and relevance.

What and How

What has been the driver for education for the past 50 years, perhaps the past 100. It has been paraphrased by the term the 3 R's – Reading, 'Riting, 'Rithmetic. The 3 R's have entered our educational lexicon as the basics of education. Basics, perhaps in order to build on, but not in basic in terms of fundamental philosophy. We have mistaken or allowed ourselves to see education as merely a content-delivery system where knowledge, or rather facts, are poured into the empty heads of unsuspecting students.

And as we have tried over the past decade to make education more business-like and accountable, we have focused myopically on the educational outcomes of guess what – reading, writing, and arithmetic.

In our haste to show progress we have halted education's growth as a sector. The *What* alone has become the rationale, the purpose, and the meat in the sausage-making of education.

> *What* we learn does have great value, but that value is created by its relationship to meaning and belonging.

What, however, only makes sense or has intrinsic value if it is aligned to the other key questions – *Why*, *Who* – and then to *Where* and *When*. *What* we learn does have great value, but that value is created by its relationship to meaning and belonging.

Similarly, *How* something is performed – whether that be a skill, a craft, or a solution – is also important but again only in the content of the purpose and relationship. *How* for many years has been relegated to solving equations that themselves often have little relevance to the learner beyond completing the task. *How*'s most positive success has been in forming the foundation for most Career and Technical Education (CTE) courses and there is much we can learn from this. Its purpose is clear, and its relationship chosen, and decided upon, often by the learner. These are examples of where a precise way of doing something (*How*) is beneficial to be learned, especially in pursuit of a specific career. The same of course would go with learning to drive, learning to swim, or learning to fly. There are good ways to do some skills and it is frequently beneficial to learn those skills.

There are however a couple of areas to debate here regarding skill development and *How*. Firstly, areas where students thrive most are areas where they have chosen the skill to be developed.

> Areas where students thrive the most are areas where they have chosen the skill to be developed.

They, the students themselves, have understood *Why* a skill is needed and *Why* it should be learned. They have already had a self-reflective discussion and seen the value. That would be the case for driving, swimming, and any of the CTE courses a student wanted to pursue.

But that is not always the case. Too often we learn skills that have little meaningful relevance beyond learning the skill. Immediate benefit may well be apparent in learning the skill – say an algebraic formula and process – but without effective and ongoing discussion and questioning, the broader purpose and value may be lost. Is a meaningful outcome of learning an algebraic expression the ability to do the equation itself or is the more meaningful outcome to experience the ability to solve problems in a structured world of numbers? In shorthand we could ask – is the skill of doing the equation itself the goal or is it the ability to solve problems?

If *How* was related to *What*, previously aligned or crafted around *Where* and *When*, and built out of *Who* and *Why*, then relevance, meaning, context, and purpose would have all been determined. For too long we have led with *What* (content) and *How* (skills) without giving them their necessary accoutrement.

Secondly, this type of skill learning is very narrowly focused. Its purpose is too often wrapped up into itself and as such doesn't account for the broader, needed skills of communication, problem solving, collaboration, and creativity. Learning *How* to do something does not have to be fixed to a specific career path or a task. It can be aligned to the broader tasks required in our ever more volatile, uncertain, complex, and ambiguous world. While the skill to remove and install plumbing may not be needed by everyone, and the skills of coding perhaps needed by a few more, the skills of problem solving will be required as a necessity by the vast majority. And problem solving can be learned in a myriad of ways, subject matter, and locations.

Notes

1   Organization for Economic Cooperation and Development (OECD), *The Future of Education and Skills 2030*, 2018.
2   Terada, Y., 'New Research Makes a Powerful Case for PBL,' *Edutopia*, February 21, 2021. www.edutopia.org/article/new-research- makes-powerful-case-pbl
3   Barron, B. & Darling-Hammond, L., 'Powerful Learning: Studies Show Deep Understanding Derives from Collaborative Methods,' *Edutopia*, October 8, 2008. www.edutopia.org/inquiry-project-learning-research
4   Bevan, B., Petrich, M., & Wilkinson, K., 'Tinkering Is Serious Play,' *Educational Leadership*, Vol. 72, No. 4 (Dec. 2014–Jan. 2015): 28–33. www.ascd.org/publications/educational-leadership/dec14/vol72/num04/Tinkering-Is-Serious-Play.aspx
5   Beesley, A., Clark, T., Barker, J., Germeroth, C., & Apthorp, H., *Expeditionary Learning Schools: Theory of Action and Literature Review of Motivation, Character, and Engagement*, McRel, 2010.
6   Hattie, J., Marsh, J., & Richards, G., 'Adventure Education and Outward Bound: Out-of-Class Experiences That Make a Lasting Difference,' *Review of Educational Research*, Vol. 67, No. 1 (1997): 43–87. https://journals.sagepub.com/doi/10.3102/00346543067001043

3

The First Step Is Always the Hardest

First Steps, First Questions

So where, or rather how, to start this journey of reframing? It does all sound too much, and too difficult, to change an entire ecosystem or educational solar system. What would I do at 8:30am on Monday morning? Would I still teach Math and if so, how? Would I follow the curriculum? What about Literature? – we are about to start a new novel.

There is always a tendency to jump into action without giving enough time to consider the issue or dilemma at hand. And there is enough evidence to show that without establishing the motivation, any change effort is doomed to failure (see *Switch* by Chip and Dan Heath). So, my first word of advice is to consider the proposition presented here. Take some time and then discuss it with others. Seek meaning and in doing so grow motivation for any change first.

> Take some time and then discuss it with others. Seek meaning and in doing so grow motivation for any change first.

DOI: 10.4324/9781003228066-5

When people push for change and it doesn't happen, they often chalk it up to lack of understanding. A mom grouses, "If my daughter just understood that her driving habits are dangerous, she'd change." A scientist says, "If we could just get Congress to understand the dangers of global warming, they'd surely take legislative action."

But when people fail to change, it's not usually because of an understanding problem. Smokers understand that cigarettes are unhealthy, but they don't quit. American automakers in the early twenty-first century knew they were too dependent on sales of SUVs and trucks (and thus on low oil prices), but they didn't innovate.

At some level, we understand this tension. We know there's a difference between knowing how to act and being motivated to act. But when it comes time to change the behavior of other people, our first instinct is to teach them something. Smoking is really unhealthy! Your chemotherapy medicine is really important! We speak to the rider when we should be speaking to the Elephant.

Heath & Heath (2011)[1]

After that start with asking questions about your classes and classrooms.

Classroom Actions and Schoolwide Discussions

Start not with changing anything about the current structure but rather start with changing and challenging your personal perspective. I wholeheartedly believe that when someone changes their view-

> Start not with changing anything about the current structure but rather start with changing and challenging your personal perspective.

point, or adjusts their mindset, their actions then change accordingly. Small changes to our purpose can illicit big changes in our actions. And like a virtuous circle one change begets another, and another.

Beyond the benchmarks, what do you want students to learn from their time with you? What do you want them to get out of this unit or this year? What personal development do you want to see flourish in your students?

Ask yourself these questions and write down the answers. Make a list and keep it by your side as you lead a lesson or plan an activity.

Follow this up by planning your questions. What we ask of our students evokes what we want them to learn. In a way, the questions we ask them showcase our reasons for having them learn something. Are we seeking mastery of content, or are we seeking perseverance? Are we expecting task completion or are we wanting to see improvements in problem solving? The questions we ask outline our intentions and set the students on their path. Ask self-reflective questions about how they are learning and what they are discovering about themselves. These don't have to be long-winded discussions, but plant the seed for introspection and self-discovery. It also begins their understanding that there may be more to what they are learning than the *What* and *How* that they are learning. It starts the unveiling of the hidden curriculum.

If they are stuck at solving or answering something, ask them what they can do to get past this rut? Have them consider their own learning at the same time that they are in the process of learning.

Every now and then, take the plunge and ask the students 'why are we learning this?' Turn the tables on them to consider

> Every now and then, take the plunge and ask the students 'why are we learning this?' Turn the tables on them to consider the answer.

the answer. Maybe they will come up with nothing beyond 'it's on the test' or 'we have to' – but maybe they will also start to consider a bigger picture embedded in the process.

We make meaning and see purpose where we can and often all we need is a reason to refocus on something to find meaning. Self-discovery – asking *Why* and *Who* – can occur as long as we are prepared to ask the questions, regardless of setting or subject area.

Then finish with asking yourself these questions:

Why did you become an educator? Why did you get into the profession in the first place?

For most of us it was an aligned belief in the power of education to develop the individual to their fullest potential and the power of education to make the world a better place. These were and are lofty goals. But somehow in the middle of our induction into teaching and our passage through the trials of accountability systems and benchmarking developed in order to make the profession more business-savvy, we have lost sight of why we entered into education in the first place. And the more we progress down this cul-de-sac, the more we become attuned to this being the norm. There is a virtue to education that has or is being lost if we don't reclaim it. There is a purpose that, if we don't state it and ask for it, will be hidden under the pile of scantron sheets and standardized test scores.

> Education is about asking and understanding *Why* and discovering *Who* we are.

Education is about asking and understanding *Why* and discovering *Who* we are. The rest, while important, revolves around these fundamental questions.

Note

1   Heath, C. & Heath, D., *Switch*, Random House Business Books, 2011, p. 113.

Part 2

Diving Deeper into Each Question and Visiting Each Planet: From Why to Who to Where and When to How and What

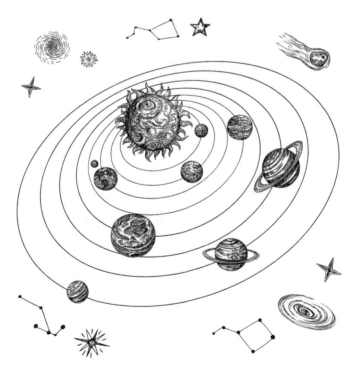

4

Why

Children, humans, are born curious. We arrive wanting and needing to learn. Watch a toddler in a garden and they are mesmerized with everything they see, hear, smell, and touch.

Then they enter school and curiosity is gradually worn down. Why? Because our schools are set up for conformity, learning things that have already been discovered, and following guidance or directions.

Children quickly discover that questioning things serves no purpose except to annoy the adult and showcase your own ignorance. It is viewed too frequently and too easily as a distraction to learning, rather than a vehicle for discovery.

> Children quickly discover that questioning things serves no purpose except to annoy the adult and showcase your own ignorance.

Take that same child back to the garden at age 7 and they may play, run, chase, but they likely won't absorb. Return again at the age of 13 and the question will be 'why are we here? What do I need to do?' all the while standing static and looking confused. It doesn't have to be this way.

We can capture that innate curiosity, harness it, and actually allow it to thrive.

DOI: 10.4324/9781003228066-7

The 2-Year-Old Dilemma

As every parent knows, many 2-year-olds go through a phase where they ask, respond, question, and requestion with the word 'why.' And what do we do? We are first amused, then frustrated, then annoyed; then after what may be days or sometimes weeks, we start retorting 'because I said so' until they stop asking why. Mission accomplished. We got them through that stage and we've effectively curtailed their curiosity. And so begins the trajectory of learning without fundamentally understanding why.

Now in truth many infants are asking why because they have learnt that this question elicits a response, and it is part of their cognitive and communicative development of action and reaction. Yet it is also true that during this time young children are also very curious as their awareness of their environment starts to grow. But whether the child is asking why because of development control or whether they are asking it because they are curious, our typical response makes sure that both agency and curiosity are nipped in the bud.

> One of the best things we can do is to capture this curiosity and nurture it. Respond to questions with answers that show that most things have a cause and effect.

One of the best things we can do is to capture this curiosity and nurture it. Respond to questions with answers that show that most things have a cause and effect. By answering we are justifying their curiosity, enhancing their understanding of the world around them, adding to their growing knowledge base, and building a relationship of shared understanding. By not answering or ceasing the dialogue, we are doing the opposite – we are letting them know curiosity is bad, information is delivered, and knowledge is fixed.

An even better response – especially as the *Why* question gets more and more specific or precise and perhaps the answer is unknown by us – is to answer with 'you know, that's a great question and I don't know. What do you think?' followed by a 'Let's try and find out.' This gives huge credibility to the question and immediately forms a bond in learning between the parent and the child. It lets them know that the world is there to be discovered and there is much that we don't know about our world. This also builds a relationship based on honesty rather than one based only on seniority.

Ask yourself – do you want your child to view the world as discoverable, where they can find out new things and form new ideas? Or do you want your child to be subdued into understanding that information is fixed and delivered?

> "The mind is not a vessel to be filled but a fire to be kindled."
>
> Plutarch[1]

> "Education is not the filling of a pail, but the lighting of a fire."
>
> W.B. Yeats[2]

Whoever uttered the above words – and it is likely that both did – the premise we take away is that a true education is one that inspires learning built on curiosity and is formed from wanting to know 'why.'

Simon Sinek, in his well-viewed TED talk 'On How Great Leaders Inspire Action,'[3] outlined the purpose or rather the need for a 'why' for every business. It's not what you're selling but rather why you're selling it. The value of a product is not only a result of its effectiveness; it is also directly related to its greater meaning or purpose. Without a why, the whole buying–selling game becomes just a transactional process where goods or services are moved from one person to another. With a why, it becomes emotive, meaningful, and dare we say, purposeful.

> We say what we do. We say how we're different or how we're better, and we expect some sort of behavior – a purchase, a vote, something like that. "Here's our new law firm. We have the best lawyers with the biggest client. We always perform for our clients. Do business with us." "Here's our new car. It gets great gas mileage. It has no leather seats. Buy our car," but it's uninspiring.

Here's how Apple actually communicates. "Everything we do, we believe in challenging the status quo. We believe in thinking differently. The way we challenge the status quo is by making our products beautifully designed, simple to use, and user-friendly. We just happen to make great computers. Wanna buy one?" Totally different, right? You're ready to buy a computer from me. All I did was reverse the order of the information.

What it proves to us is that people don't buy what you do, people buy why you do it. People don't buy what you do, they buy why you do it.

Sinek (2009)[4]

In education, just as we taught the 2-year-old to shy away from asking why, we have become experts at reciting or regurgitating facts and content. And it's not just the students; teachers have also – too often – become compliant because of how the system has been developed. We too often recite or regurgitate *What* we do or *How* we do it without considering *Why* we do it.

We debate endlessly, and often furiously, the *How* and the *What* – Language Arts versus Science; Physical Education compared to Music; extra study time or recess; play or instruction; seat time against project-based learning; standardized testing in competition with portfolios; scripted curriculum or differentiated instruction; common core or site-level control, and so forth, and so forth.

> All these debates, arguments, and shoutfests are meaningless – or, at best, dysfunctional – unless we first determine *Why* we have education.

But all these debates, arguments, and shoutfests are meaningless – or, at best, dysfunctional – unless we first determine *Why* we have education.

From this *Why*, all other vehicles, processes, subjects, themes, curricula, and techniques – all the *Whats* and *Hows* – can be sorted.

However, this flies in the face of research that shows when people understand the purpose of what's being learnt they learn more and more effectively, and they also enjoy the learning.

We seek meaning. We desire purpose. But we educate our children via a system that treats understanding why as at best a luxury. It is something that is reserved for the debating club or the

We seek meaning. We desire purpose. But we educate our children via a system that treats understanding why as at best a luxury.

philosophy class. The proverbial cherry on top of the sundae, the reward for hard work, the extra as opposed to the required.

But what would happen to our system and our students' learning if we started with *Why*. We would slow the amount of content being taught down, but we would increase the value of that learning.

We would ourselves have to justify – or rather determine for ourselves initially – what value something has to be learned. It may not be, and in fact often wouldn't

We would slow the amount of content being taught down, but we would increase the value of that learning.

be, the mere learning of content that's important, but rather the act of learning or debating or discovering or persevering.

What Was Then Required Is Now Optional

While we hold up foundations of knowledge, and core texts or formulae, as being sacrosanct, the truth is that we have consistently, though not always constantly, adjusted and altered what is taught. This process was, and is, tied to the ever-growing and increasing amount of information out there. As such we have seen changes – or at least debates about changes – expand exponentially in recent years as the amount of information in our world increases exponentially.

Up until 1960, both Oxford and Cambridge, and the majority of universities in the UK, required Latin as a prerequisite for entrance to any undergraduate course. The premise was that this subject formed the basis of our language and such of our understandings of the world; hence for anyone in a university to be considered educated, they must have at least the basis of this seminal subject area.

The virtues of Latin can be argued as it does form the basis for much of our world across literature, science, and philosophy. Yet both Oxford and Cambridge, along with the vast majority of all universities, have done away with this as a general requirement, unless of course it relates directly to the area of study. The reasoning is, as summarized in 1917 by former Harvard President, Charles William Eliot, that there "are too many histories, too many new sciences with applications of great importance, and too many new literatures of high merit which have a variety of modern uses, to permit anyone, not bound to the classics by affectionate associations and educational tradition, to believe that Latin can maintain the place it has held for centuries in the youthful training of educated men, a place which it acquired when it was the common speech of scholars and has held for centuries without any such good reason."[5]

Oxford and Cambridge both did away with Latin as a prerequisite in 1960.[6] Most US universities and colleges, including Yale and Harvard, had done away with Latin and Greek as a prerequisite by the 1930s and 1940s.[7]

[T]he idea of the cultivated person, man or woman, has distinctly changed during the past thirty-five years. Cultivation a generation ago meant acquaintance with letters and the fine arts, and some knowledge of at least two languages and literatures, and of history. The term 'cultivation' is now much more inclusive. It includes elementary knowledge of the sciences, and it ranks high the subjects of history, government, and economics.

Eliot (1917)[8]

These writings, extolling the fact that there were now too many new things to be learned to focus primarily on Latin or Greek, were made in 1917 prior to the end of World War One, prior to the rise of fascism or communism, prior to World War Two, the atomic bomb, the cure for polio, the first heart transplant, the first man on the moon, the invention of the computer, the internet, or the iPhone.

In the short space of time between when the iPhone was released on January 9, 2007 to today, the amount of information has not only more than doubled; it has likely doubled many millions of times over.

> The amount of information has not only more than doubled; it has likely doubled many millions of times over.

In fact, when researching this section it was almost impossible to get an accurate figure, and considering the fact that information is being created as we read (or as I type), everything becomes outdated very quickly. The premise is that there is much more information out there than there was even a year ago and an insanely larger amount that before the iPhone. Let's not even consider going back to how much information was out there before the internet.

Buckminster Fuller, the American architect, futurist, author, designer, and inventor, coined the notion of the 'knowledge doubling curve' (Fuller, 1981),[9] which stated that while human knowledge had doubled at a general rate of every century up until 1900, it had quickened to a rate of doubling every 25 years by 1945. By 2020, according to an IBM report, human knowledge would double every 12 hours, fueled by the Internet of Things

(Schilling 2013).[10] As stated by Paul Chamberlain, in 'Knowledge is Not Everything':

> Arguably we may have reached a point where relevant knowledge is increasing faster and in greater quantities than we can absorb. However, while knowledge is increasing, the useful lifespan of knowledge is decreasing. Consequently, we need to be constantly replacing out-of-date knowledge with new knowledge in a continuous process of unlearning and learning. Knowledge alone however is not sufficient and as important is the ability to apply good judgement based on knowledge... what we know as wisdom. It is knowledge and wisdom put into action that gives us insight.
>
> Chamberlain (2020)[11]

We are no longer able to deliver all the content knowledge that is available to us, as this information is doubling at an astounding rate.

The speed of change is forcing us, whether we like it or not, to upend our education systems. We are no longer able to deliver all the content knowledge that is available to us, as this information is doubling at an astounding rate.

Even if we wanted to keep *What* as our core or central star, the chance of us being able to keep up with the informational overload is impossible.

In 2013, I gave a talk on the *Future of Education* at the 1st International Conference on Values in Buenos Aries, Argentina. Part of the talk was focused around showcasing the exponential growth of information that we were (are) experiencing and was based on the video 'Did You Know?.'[12] The video, released originally in 2009, highlighted the speed of information growth across the world. It talked about how we are now competing with India for jobs in this global environment. It talked about personal computers and how they are taking over core parts of our lives from the professional to the personal.

It talked about social networking and the growth of personal pages online. It talked about MySpace, not Facebook. It declared that "[i]f MySpace was a country it would be the 11th-largest in the world (between Japan and Mexico)." At the time of writing (March 2021), Facebook has 2.7 billion users, making it not only larger than any country globally but equal to both the most populous countries, China and India, combined. Or to put it another way, it is equal to the populations of the next 20 countries combined (United States, Indonesia, Pakistan, Brazil, Nigeria, Bangladesh, Russia, Mexico, Japan, Ethiopia, Philippines, Egypt, Vietnam, DR Congo, Turkey, Iran, Germany, Thailand, United Kingdom, France). Not bad growth for a company that wasn't highlighted as a key social network in 2009.

What struck me at the time of my talk was that the video didn't mention Twitter. Twitter was launched in 2006, and in 2009 when the video was produced Twitter wasn't really a thing. On the day of my presentation in 2013, and just four years later, Twitter went public. A company that was in its infancy in 2009 and didn't rate a mention was suddenly worth $14.2 billion. Twitter as of 2021 has over 330 million monthly users.

The video also didn't mention the iPhone. It didn't mention Netflix. It didn't mention Tesla. It didn't mention cryptocurrencies. And there is a good chance in our current world that by the short time that this manuscript gets published there will be another selection of companies that have risen from seemingly nowhere. Growth is fast and getting faster.

The amount of information out there is increasing exponentially, and it would be a fool's errand to try to teach – in the older sense of the word – all relevant information. It is a much better use of our time and that of our children and youth to help them learn not a set of essential facts and figures but rather the competencies, skills, and attributes that allow them to learn and be continuously curious about their world and themselves.

> It is a much better use of our time and that of our children and youth to help them learn not a set of essential facts and figures but rather the competencies, skills, and attributes that allow them to learn and be continuously curious about their world and themselves.

Learning Too Many Things Because We Haven't Been Taught to Ask Why

Every country is going through the same debate. They are battling the unanswerable question of how do we compete with the growth of information and at the same time make learning more personal and meaningful? It is a battle between the content-warriors and the pedagogists. How can we personalize learning, how can we develop the skills of problem solving, creativity, even empathy in our children when our curriculum is so overloaded? This discussion is being had from Norway to Estonia, from Australia to Singapore, from Canada to Brazil. From the offices of the OECD (Organization for Economic Cooperation and Development) to the school boards in British Columbia. What do we jettison if we are to take time for these newer competencies? Because we can't go on – successfully or effectively – as we are currently.

> What do we jettison if we are to take time for these newer competencies? Because we can't go on – successfully or effectively – as we are currently.

The problem is that we haven't truly begun to ask ourselves why we have an education system and what we want to get out of it. We have to a certain extent abdicated our collective responsibility to politicians to determine what our educational purpose is. And those politicians by and large have followed the lead of other politicians globally.

Pasi Sahlberg, the Finnish educator, coined the phrase Global Education Reform Movement (GERM) to explain this. It captures how a pro testing and accountability phase for education spread from the US via its No Child Left Behind Act (2001)[13] to the educational frameworks of the UK, the Netherlands, and Germany, to Australia and New Zealand. The acronym-as-analogy worked as it described a phenomenon that Sahlberg identified as "like an epidemic that spreads and infects education systems through a virus" (Sahlberg, 2012).[14] GERM showed us how educational policy gets implemented and embedded into countries and systems; too often it is merely replicated from one country to another based on little more than political opportunism. It was a race to move up the PISA ranking (Programme for International Student Assessment)[15] and to do it quickly. This was in contradiction to the fact that both the highfliers in PISA – Finland and Singapore – had implemented long-term generational change initiatives in their educational systems for which they were both now seeing results. It didn't matter that the effects of the No Child Left Behind Act – well-intentioned but ultimately flawed – was greater student disengagement, teacher demoralization, and the disintegration of public trust in education. What mattered was a quick turnaround in the global educational league table rankings for short-term political gain.

Educating our children and youth cannot be for short-term political gain and nor can it be implemented without truly discussing why it is there in the first place. The answer, even for our systems, must come from reframing the foundation of education away from *What* and *How* to *Why*.

> Educating our children and youth cannot be for short-term political gain and nor can it be implemented without truly discussing why it is there in the first place.

Purpose Seeking Clarity

Alvin Toffler, futurist and author of the book *Future Shock* (1970),[16] suggested that: "Tomorrow's illiterate will not be the man who can't read; he will be the man who has not learned how to learn." That quote, from a half century ago comes from a discussion with psychologist Herbert Gerjuoy. Others have expanded this quote to mean that we will need to be learning, unlearning, and relearning, and suggested that there will soon be use-by dates on knowledge or information. That is not to necessarily say that the information will be incorrect but rather that it will become old, irrelevant, or obsolete.

Similarly, Marc Rosenberg stated in 'The Coming Knowledge Tsunami':

> [A]n even bigger issue is how long it takes for knowledge to become outdated, incorrect, or irrelevant. One measure of this is the half-life of knowledge, the amount of time it takes for knowledge to lose half its value. For many content domains, especially in science, technology, Research and Development, marketing, and even finance, the half-life of knowledge is shrinking. Information that 10 years ago was useful for 12 months might only be valuable for 6 months today.
>
> Rosenberg (2017)[17]

> We are faced with both too much information and little idea of how to gauge its usefulness.

We are faced with both too much information and little idea how to gauge its usefulness. Facts, content, and information should become tools of learning – to be utilized when and as needed. And *What* is to be learned must be continuously reviewed, replaced, or updated as needed dependent upon the desired outcomes of the learning.

So, what are the desired outcomes of the learning? Sometimes it will be mastery of a skill, understanding of a concept, or a precise series of facts. But that cannot and should not be assumed.

We must start with reigniting discussions around what our core purpose is in education. We must seek clarity by dissecting our purpose or purposes. This however is something that we have at best ill considered, and at worst have ignored.

There is scant evidence that much trickles down from our well-meaning and beautifully crafted mission statements in education. Too often any prose or purpose is lost the moment we hold up and compare the mission with the syllabus. What was once well meaning quickly becomes irrelevant as we refocus our teaching upon the bible of the benchmark. Our aim and purpose quickly become interlocked and intertwined as we seek not to raise and fulfill each child's potential to be global citizens but to instead achieve annual yearly progress on set of test scores measured via a multiple-choice scantron sheet. Any debates at how such outcomes stack up against our mission statements are rarely held and the educational machine, designed not for raising potential but for achieving better test scores, moves on.

> There is scant evidence that much trickles down from our well-meaning and beautifully crafted mission statements in education.

Before we start to ask each individual educator to rethink what they do, or at least why they do it, we must start with the profession itself. Until we can come to greater clarity on our overall purpose as a system – whether that be academic attainment, personal development, citizenship, community, or societal engagement; the list could go on – we will stimy reform and the most well-meaning of teachers' endeavors.

I am not here to debate the purpose – though I certainly have my views, many of which do eke out throughout this book – but I am here to insist that we have the debate. Why do we have an education system and what do we want our students to gain from it?

It sounds simple and straightforward enough, but we don't have this discussion because we are afraid of the answers. What do we do if we decide that much of *What* is taught is a waste, obsolete, or more likely, indirectly related to what we intend our outcomes to be? Like an injury or illness that needs to be addressed or fixed before it gets worse and irreparable, we must start the process of asking ourselves *Why* we have an education system in order to then fix, ameliorate, or adjust what we are currently doing because what we are currently doing is on its last legs.

> . . . we can teach much of what is likely needed – such as creativity, problem solving, ingenuity, empathy, communication, resilience – via a myriad of subject matter or investigative projects.

I am guessing, and you're probably not too surprised to hear this, that we are going to find that we don't need to make radical changes to the content or skills necessarily, nor immediately, but we do need to change the questions we are asking ourselves and our students as they learn. The reason for this is that we can teach much of what is likely needed – such as creativity, problem solving, ingenuity, empathy, communication, resilience – via a myriad of subject matter or investigative projects.

The vehicles are less important than the outcomes discovered and developed during the process.

As we begin our questioning of the profession itself, and by process the purpose of each subject area or learning pathway, we will become better and better at linking value and relationships back to our intended outcomes.

Ask yourself: when was the last time you discussed the purpose of education or the purpose of your specific teaching area with colleagues? My guess is never or perhaps seldom. Math has a functional purpose but after middle school what is the core reason? Certainly, it's a path to certain careers but should it also be considered as a vehicle that allows us to train abstract thinking but with clear unambiguous answers? Should Math also be considered similar to a language that allows new divergent thinking to take place and spark new understandings of both our abilities but also our world?

There are a myriad of ways that every subject area can develop what we desire from an education system and even more ways when we align and collaborate across subject areas. The issue is that we haven't clearly asked ourselves *Why* and subsequently what outcomes we are seeking. And those that haven't been asked should not be expected to have the answers, or at least not immediately. Let's start by asking *Why* and then let's evolve our understandings from what those responses are. There is a very good chance that the first response may be 'I don't know.'

The Beauty of IDK

'I don't know' is viewed as a negative. Teachers are meant to know, well, everything – from why this subject is important, to why the sky is blue, to how to find cotangent and cosecant angles. Yet the best teachers aren't necessarily the ones that know the most facts; they are more often the ones that can relate and make the learning meaningful to their students. 'I don't know' can and should be viewed rather as an opportunity to learn and a path to make the learning relevant.

'I don't know' can and should be viewed as a positive step in the learning process. Many teachers are already starting to do this. From co-learning or collaborative learning through to co-creation, we are beginning this process by asking why. Why are we learning this and what do we want to learn? We are, albeit slowly, moving from that 'sage on the stage' to the 'guide on the side.' It's been at least 40 years since that phrase was uttered – Alice Johnson in 1981 was the earliest I found[18] – but education reform is one of the slowest of slow trains.

> 'I don't know' can and should be viewed as a positive step in the learning process.

Collaborative learning is gaining traction across classrooms and schools as teachers utilize the knowledge and curiosity of the students to foster learning. Doug Fischer and Nancy Frey highlight collaborative learning as a step towards the gradual release of responsibility from the teacher to the student, where "students are expected to apply the skills and knowledge they have been taught and to turn to one another for support and enrichment. As they interact with one another, learning moves forward, and students use a number of soft skills—communication, leadership, negotiation—that take on increased importance" (Fisher & Frey, 2014).[19]

As students gain more experience, they also gain more ownership of the learning. Collaborative learning can occur most easily from peer-to-peer, student-to-student, but it can also occur from student-to-teacher. What has occurred in many classrooms during the Covid-19 pandemic, and subsequent transition to online and hybrid learning, has been a gradual blurring of the lines between student and teacher. This new online environment has allowed many students, who were more adept at online platforms, to be able to guide and upskill other students and staff, and has helped foster a shared responsibility and shared ownership for learning.

> This journey to shared ownership often starts with a simple 'I don't know.'

This journey to shared ownership often starts with a simple 'I don't know.' It starts with the same attitude that we had when our 2-year-old asked why. 'I don't know but let's find out.' Teachers aren't owners of knowledge and especially nowadays with the outrageous influx of content, information, and ideas, they cannot be. What they are, and what they must be, are nurturers and guides to learning. They must be pedagogical experts, not walking Siris.

What gets relayed when we say 'I don't know'? It tells the learner that there is information out there that we can learn. It tells them that the process of learning is ongoing. It tells them that learning is a lifelong activity. It tells them that anyone can learn. And it tells them that there are processes that we can use to learn new things.

All of these messages open the door to learning. They tell the learner that information is not owned by anyone but rather is fluid, changing, and obtainable. They tell the learner that there is always a process for learning and in doing so promotes a growth mindset. They tell the learner that understanding these processes will allow anyone to learn anywhere and anytime. And they tell the learner that curiosity is both valued and at the core of all true learning.

> . . . they tell the learner that curiosity is both valued and at the core of all true learning.

'I don't know' is a powerful statement. It diffuses and equalizes the teacher–student relationship. It forms a relationship based on learning. It admits humility and builds respect. It automatically does more than any lesson plan to move from that Sage on the Stage to the Guide on the Side.

Interestingly, this is also becoming a more common stance and approach outside of the education world. The era of 'old-school professionalism' where the boss knows the answer to everything and directs the company like a ship's captain is waning. Instead, companies are viewing their organizations as teams that can respond and react to situations via collaborative leadership and what has been called 'messy leadership' – leading with empathy, leading with compassion, and leading with uncertainty.

In a recent article with *Entrepreneur* magazine, Jerry Connor, Head of Leadership Practice at BTS – a leadership development company focused on the people side of strategy – outlined this approach.

> We found that leaders who struggled the most during the crisis were those who fell victim to "superhero syndrome," or wanting to put on a brave face for their employees to project strength and expertise. Leaders who were well-respected in normal times found their people looking to them for guidance, but this only created bottlenecks and inhibited creativity. When the pace of change became too fast for them to lead from the front as they always had, many tried to compensate by working longer, unsustainable hours.
>
> In contrast, the leaders who were able to weather the crisis best were those with the confidence to take themselves out of the driver's seat and admit that they didn't have all the answers. They were willing to let go of their attachment to driving outcomes—choosing, instead, to embody vulnerability, humility and trust.
>
> Connor (2021)[20]

In full disclosure, this author currently heads the education non-profit of the BTS company. It is remarkable though that as we hear so much talk in and across education that we need to become more business-like, we are at the same time seeing businesses become more people-centric, able to adjust to ambiguity, and willing to step off that stage.

Business-like to the education community equates to taking the human out of the operation. It means being directed by data – a purely objective world where emotion and human traits are not part of the equation. Nothing against data per se but it shouldn't and mustn't be the omnipresent force that means the human side of teaching, pedagogy, and decision making is left out. We are able to apply data (i.e., in the form of numbers, charts, and trend line tables) in certain aspects of our profession but it doesn't explain the whole process, nor the whole beauty, of learning.

> These points of data become designated national landmarks that we are all now meant to direct our attention towards and swoon over.

> Being data driven actually moves us closer to being data obsessed and data blinkered.

These points of data become designated national landmarks that we are all now meant to direct our attention towards and swoon over. The fragrance industry has coined the phrase 'nose-blind,' just as we in the education community run the risk of becoming 'data-blind.'

Being data driven actually moves us closer to being data obsessed and data blinkered. We don't see what we don't see and the whole system is off and running down another rabbit hole of obscure, somewhat applicable, yet more often irrelevant data. We've done this dance before, whether it be standardized test scores that illuminate the necessary information, such as the underrepresentation of minority populations in advanced courses, but obscure the true purpose of education and obsess the politicians. Or the recent infatuation with 3rd grade reading levels. Again, this focus illuminates areas of need, adjustment, and remediation, but it also makes the process and system take a sharp turn towards teaching to the test, and focusing on the data outcomes of what can be measured. An analogy would be focusing all our attention on the upcoming hurdle in a steeplechase while ignoring the fact that after that we have another seven laps to go. Yes, we want every student (runner) to get over the first hurdle but we don't want to tire everyone out just as the race has started, or even worse have them question why they ever joined the race in the first place.

I prefer to follow what Andy Hargreaves and Dennis Shirley call 'data informed' as opposed to 'data driven.' In this scenario, the data adds to the conversation and shines light on the learning taking place, informing but not directing the pedagogy. In the aptly named article 'Data-Driven to Distraction,' they explain the issue with being 'data driven':

> Teachers are no longer the drivers of reform, but the driven. Many teachers and schools, in fact, are being driven to distraction. Under the pressures of the federal No Child Left Behind Act and its mandate for "adequate yearly progress," teachers in struggling schools are being told that only results matter—and even these rarely extend beyond tested achievement in literacy and math....
>
> Data-driven instruction obliterates the crucial fact that to be effective, educators have to use many different kinds of information to think about what they are doing in classrooms. While statistics can be immensely useful, they do not automatically point to which instructional approaches will work best with the diverse learners that make up a school's classes, or a nation's schools. One child may struggle with under-performance because she has difficulties with reading, a second because he has a turbulent home life, and a third because she is a recent immigrant learning English as a second language. Faced with such diversity, teachers and educational leaders have to be intelligently informed by evidence, not blindly driven by it to teach a certain way...
>
> Hargreaves & Shirley (2006)[21]

At the same time that we in education try to become more 'business-like,' the business community is striving to become more 'human.' Looking to understand how the emotional, connective, relational side of us all impacts their companies. It's a switch of intention and an appreciation of how complex yet intertwined all of us are.

A recent edition of the Korn Ferry *Briefings Magazine*, put out by one of the leading human resources and organizational consulting firms, highlights this with a focus on *The Human Touch*.[22] The edition touched on ways that successful businesses are tapping into the human side of the work, their staff, and their customers, extolling the benefits of social impact, connecting with people on a personal level, and developing the ethos (culture) of their workplace.

A lead in one of the stories was Brian McNamara, CEO of GlaxoSmithKline Consumer Healthcare, the world's largest consumer healthcare company, which serves 1.5 billion people a year through brands such as Sensodyne, Advil, and Centrum.

> "At GSK, like many large companies, at times we can be a bit bureaucratic and central in the way we think about things," says McNamara, who took the reins in 2016. But as COVID-19 swept across the globe, he recognized that leaders had to empower local management to make real-time decisions and eliminate nonessential planning. GSK set three priorities: caring for its people, ensuring business continuity, and being part of the solution… "When personal purpose and company purpose connect, man, everything just becomes so much easier."[23]

Neither Korn Ferry nor GlaxoSmithKline are alone in this human endeavor. Scroll through recent editions of other leading for-profit directed business magazines finds similar approaches.

◆ *Forbes* – 'Be Human First: The Robot-Proof Human Trifecta,' June 24, 2021[24]

◆ *Forbes* – 'How to Treat Customers as Humans Instead of Numbers: 14 Expert Tips,' June 17, 2021[25]

◆ *Forbes* – 'More Humans Should Be More Human. Practice These 3 Must-Have Human Skills for Leading Hybrid Teams!,' June 15, 2021[26]

◆ *Harvard Business Review*, 'The Fundamental Human Relationship with Work,' October 13, 2020[27]

◆ *Harvard Business Review* – 'Don't Let Digital Transformation Make You Less Human,' May 20, 2020[28]

If anything, it seems that the pandemic of 2020–21 has rewired a societal focus on being human. Business seems to be taking up the challenge and let's hope that education reasserts it appreciation of its distinctly human side and human purpose.

If anything, it seems that the pandemic of 2020–2021 has rewired a societal focus on being human.

We cannot shirk the human side of our work as our work is inherently human and relational. We ignore the person at our own risk, and at the risk of our profession. We create bonds between learning and the learner, and we grow meaning through understanding – understanding the purpose (*Why*), but also understanding the individual (*Who*). We are a human-based and human-propelled profession.

Why in the Classroom

Questions to ask yourself
- Why did I become an educator?
- Why did I get into the profession in the first place?
- Do I still believe this to be true? If not, why not?
- What do I want my students to gain from my efforts?

Questions to ask your students
- What have you learned to do this [topic/unit/activity] that surprised you?
- What would you like to learn from our time together this year? Don't restrict to answers to only content (*What*) or skills (*How*).

Questions for your students to ask themselves
- We require children to go to school for 9–12 years. Why do we do this? What do we want them to develop?
- What in our current school system helps this?
- If you were inventing a school from scratch, what would you start with and focus on?

Notes

1   Plutarch quote, via *GoodReads*. www.goodreads.com/quotes/ 32595-the-mind-is-not-a-vessel-to-be-filled-but

2   W.B. Yeats quote, via *Irish Times*. www.irishtimes.com/news/education/education-is-not-the-filling-of-a-pail-but-the-lighting-of-a-fire-it-s-an-inspiring-quote-but-did-wb-yeats-say-it-1.1560192

3   Sinek, S., 'On How Great Leaders Inspire Action', *TEDx* talk, 2009. www.ted.com/talks/simon_sinek_how_great_leaders_inspire_action.html

4   Sinek, S., Ibid.

5   Eliot, C.W., 'The Case Against Compulsory Latin', *The Atlantic*, 1917. www.theatlantic.com/magazine/archive/1917/03/the-case-against-compulsory-latin/543222/

6   Forest, M., 'The Abolition of Compulsory Latin and Its Consequences', *Greece & Rome*, Vol. 50 (2003): 42–66. www.jstor.org/stable/3567835

7   Lafleur, R.A., 'The Classical Languages and College Admissions: An American Classical League Survey', *The Classical Outlook*, Vol. 68, No. 4 (Summer 1991): 124–132. www.jstor.org/stable/43937115

8   Eliot, C.W., Ibid.

9   Fuller, R.B., *Critical Path*, St. Martin's Press, 1981.

10 Schilling, D.R., 'Knowledge Doubling Every 12 Months, Soon to be Every 12 Hours', *Industry Tap*, April 19, 2013. www.industrytap.com/knowledge-doubling-every-12-months-soon-to-be-every-12-hours/3950

11 Chamberlain, P., 'Knowledge is Not Everything', *Design for Health*, Vol. 4, No. 1 (2020): 1–3. https://doi.org/10.1080/24735132.2020.1731203

12 'Did You Know?' 2009, via YouTube. www.youtube.com/watch?v=AUiObUYEBKc

13 No Child Left Behind Act, 2001. www.congress.gov/bill/107th-congress/house-bill/1

14 Sahlberg, P. 'How GERM Is Infecting Schools Around the World?' 2012. https://pasisahlberg.com/text-test/

15 Programme for International Student Assessment (PISA). www.oecd.org/pisa/

16 Toffler, A.. *Future Shock* (18th ed.), Harvard, 1970, p. 414.

17 Rosenberg, M., 'The Coming Knowledge Tsunami', October 10, 2017, *Learning Solutions*. https://learningsolutionsmag.com/articles/2468/marc-my-words-the-coming-knowledge-tsunami

18 *Harlan Daily Enterprise*, August 6, 1981. https://news.google.com/newspapers?id=CkhBAAAAIBAJ&sjid=6qgMAAAAIBAJ&pg=4882,4948961&dq=sage-on-the-stage&hl=en

19 Fischer, D. & Frey, N., *Better Learning Through Structured Teaching: A Framework for the Gradual Release of Responsibility* (2nd ed.), ASCD, 2014, p. 66.

20 Connor, J., 'Why "Messy" Leaders are the Future', April 7, 2021, *Entrepreneur*. www.entrepreneur.com/article/368187

21 Hargreaves, A. & Shirley, D., 'Data-Driven to Distraction', October 3, 2006, *Education Week*. www.edweek.org/technology/opinion-data-driven-to-distraction/2006/10

22 Korn Ferry *Briefings Magazine*, 'The Human Touch.' www.kornferry.com/insights/briefings-magazine/issue-49/human-touch

23 Korn Ferry *Briefings Magazine*, Ibid.

24 *Forbes Magazine*, 'Be Human First: The Robot-Proof Human Trifecta,' June 24, 2021. www.forbes.com/sites/forbesbusinesscouncil/2021/06/24/be-human-first-the-robot-proof-human-trifecta

25 *Forbes Magazine*, 'How to Treat Customers as Humans Instead of Numbers: 14 Expert Tips,' June 17, 2021. www.forbes.com/sites/forbescoachescouncil/2021/06/17/how-to-treat-customers-as-humans-instead-of-numbers-14-expert-tips

26 *Forbes Magazine*, 'More Humans Should Be More Human. Practice These 3 Must-Have Human Skills for Leading Hybrid Teams!,' June 15, 2021. www.forbes.com/sites/teresahopke/2021/06/15/more-humans-should-be-more-human-practice-these-3-must-have-human-skills-for-leading-hybrid-teams

27 *Harvard Business Review*, 'The Fundamental Human Relationship with Work', October 13, 2020. https://hbr.org/podcast/2020/10/the-fundamental-human-relationship-with-work

28 *Harvard Business Review*, 'Don't Let Digital Transformation Make You Less Human,' May 20, 2020. https://hbr.org/2020/05/dont-let-digital-transformation-make-you-less-human

5

Who

Why is critical and by placing why as a fundamental basis for education it answers many questions around purpose and meaning. But equally fundamental is the premise that education is there to help us find out more about ourselves – both *Who* we are and may want to become. But it is also about answering *Who* we (plural) are and may want to become.

By exploring and challenging different aspects of ourselves, we both expand the notion of who we are and at the same time solidify who we are. The more we discover and discuss ourselves, the more we become in tune with our own being.

> The more we discover and discuss ourselves, the more we become in tune with our own being.

Education has been held up as a way to allow children to discover their own potential and discover aspects about themselves that may otherwise remain hidden. The Montessori philosophy exemplifies this by encouraging children to learn for themselves via classrooms and activities that guide and promote self-discovery, placing the child at the center and allowing them to lead their own learning.

> The child has to acquire physical independence by being self-sufficient; he must become of independent will by using in freedom his own power of choice; he must become capable of independent thought by working

DOI: 10.4324/9781003228066-8

alone without interruption. The child's development follows a path of successive stages of independence, and our knowledge of this must guide us in our behaviour towards him. We have to help the child to act, will and think for himself. This is the art of serving the spirit, an art which can be practised to perfection only when working among children.

Montessori (1969)[1]

Non-Montessori schools also do this regularly, but perhaps less deliberately, as part of the regular school-day by providing a range of opportunities to try new activities, learn new skills, and practice new understandings, and allowing each child to learn more about themselves.

The vast majority of students thrust into a Drama class and onto the stage will likely not perform throughout their lives but what this activity does do is push our understanding of what we are capable of. It frequently increases our own self-efficacy and changes our self-concept. It broadens our horizons of what is possible by showing us that there is more to us than we first assumed.

Such realizations are frequent via the Arts as they engage students in activities that they may not have been accustomed to. But they can also happen in Physical Education, Math, the Humanities, or the Sciences. It's often less about what you are learning, and more how you are learning it, that evokes these personal reflections and appreciations.

Some subjects or learning environments, though, do help the process. Outdoor Education has long been a vehicle where students are able to discover more about themselves and change any fixed notion that they may have had. It provides platforms where the student can engage in what appear to be risk-taking activities but are in fact very safe and secure. The activities take you purposefully out of your comfort zone and place you in situations of 'perceived risk.' Whether it's zip lining, rock climbing, abseiling, or even hiking, these activities hold the potential to change our notion of what we are capable of and what we enjoy.

The same results can occur from any new subject matter, skill, or activity but are more likely to occur when we are pushed out of our familiar settings and outside areas of strength.

Author Tom Hoerr, when he was principal at The New School in St. Louis, would deliberately plan the learning around the multiple intelligences coined by Howard Gardner. The thinking was that as we each have stronger and weaker intelligences, we can promote learning by initially targeting the intelligences that we are most adept at. Whether it be logical-mathematical, linguistic, interpersonal or intrapersonal, musical or visual, kinesthetic or even naturalist, we each have a preference or tendency towards learning in a certain way. This is not unlike what occurs during personalized learning where we focus on a student's interests, preferences, and skills.

But Hoerr and his school would also do something different. Once a student mastered what was needed via their strongest intelligence, the school would have them focus on their weakest intelligence. So, if you were less-linguistic or less-musical you would be taught via this intelligence. What this did was twofold. Firstly, it had the student experience difficulty in learning something via a method that was not easy or automatic for them. It caused them to have to struggle and persevere. Secondly, it changed many students' under-standing of themselves. What they thought they were not skilled at they soon found out they were capable of. It changed the students' perception of themselves from being 'I'm good at this but poor at that' to 'I'm good at many things and I am able to learn new things.'

> It changed the students' perception of themselves from being 'I'm good at this but poor at that' to 'I'm good at many things and I am able to learn new things.'

The students' perception of who they are had changed.[2]

Personalized Learning and the Rise of the Individual

In more recent years, and across mainstream schools in many countries, we have seen the rise of personalized learning where the curriculum, the activities, and at times, the methods for assessment, are adjusted to suit the learners' interests and needs. In 2005, UK educationalist Dan Buckley defined personalized learning as being along a continuum from 'Learning tailored for the learner' and 'Learning tailored by the learner,'[3] and while definitions have ebbed and flowed to include/exclude individualized learning or differentiation, the continuum from 'tailored for' to 'tailored by' still resonates. It outlines the progression from some control, choice, and voice through to greater empowerment. As the pedagogical methods move along the continuum, they empower the learner with greater ownership and address an expanding array of decisions based on the individual's learning style.

As the learner moves from a selection of choices, to choosing the learning themselves, they are evolving their understanding of themselves, and at the same framing what they can do. Such learning environments are dually beneficial for not only self-awareness but also self-development.

> As the learner moves from a selection of choices to choosing the learning themselves, they are evolving their understanding of themselves, and at the same framing what they can do.

Just as with everything in education, personalized learning can mean different things to different people in practice, though the central understanding of it as reframing learning to be more specific and personalized to the needs of the learner remains the same. It can involve the 'engineering model' of personalized learning that emphasizes mastery of some predetermined set of academic content with personalization coming in as the teacher adjusts or adapts the learning to suit the level and needs of that learner. It can include a greater focus on adapting and adjusting what is being taught (*What* and *How*) to suit the interests and needs of the learner. It can also encompass situations where students themselves are leading the learning choices, or co-creating learning experiences, where the content isn't necessarily driving the effort. The skill of the teacher in such circumstances is that of a pedagogical expert, designing and crafting learning paths to suit the interest and abilities of each student.

> Personalization at its core means adjusting to the needs and interests of the learner and from that point the process can expand to include all aspects that make learning more specific and meaningful to the individual.

Personalization at its core means adjusting to the needs and interests of the learner and from that point the process can expand to include all aspects that make learning more specific and meaningful to the individual. As you can imagine the rise of technology has played, and is playing, a big role in making personalization more mainstream. Whether it is the ability of programs to determine current knowledge and gaps and then present students with a learning path that addresses their individual needs, or the enhanced accessibility for each student to source information for a self-directed learning project, technology is moving the personalization drive and making it both easier and more commonplace.

And if anything, the Covid-19 pandemic has helped spark this interest (and indeed need) for greater personalization. As Geoff Spencer outlined in 'Schools after COVID-19: From a Teaching Culture to a Learning Culture':

> The uniform is one size too big. The shoes need breaking in. The brand-new backpack hangs awkwardly off a pair of tiny shoulders. There's a brave smile with a missing tooth or two, a final holding of hands, a hug, a kiss, a hesitant wave, and inevitable tears.
>
> Before COVID-19 disrupted our lives and forced our kids to open their laptops and learn from home, the first day of school was a rite of passage—the start of a life-determining journey that has broadly followed the same shape and rhythm for generations.
>
> From kindergarten to Year 12, classrooms are run by teachers who deliver lessons that start and end with a

bell. They set tests, watch over examinations, and post grades that might delight, disappoint, or even surprise parents.

This one-size-fits-all approach to education has been in place for a couple of hundred years. Now, however, it is undergoing unprecedented change and not just because of COVID.

The response to the coronavirus has demonstrated how technology can help transform how we teach and learn. But the push for change started long before the pandemic struck, and it will go on long after the threat subsides. For years, policymakers have been exploring new transformative approaches to K-12 education that go far beyond just online lessons at home.

Spencer (2020)[4]

And where it is helping most, according to Geoff Spencer, is in changing our attitudes of and about education, moving it from "a teaching culture to a learning culture."[5]

We are re–situating the student at the center of the learning equation and adjusting our teaching (and their learning) to suit. There has been a necessary acceptance by many teachers to allow for greater student autonomy, greater choice and voice, greater agency and owner-ship, and decision making. There has been a growing appreci-ation over the past year to both allow for greater autonomy in learning and curate what is being learned to suit the students, as a result of these unforeseen circumstances and new learning environments.

> We are re-situating the student at the center of the learning equation and adjusting our teaching (and their learning) to suit.

Covid-19 and the school year of 2019–2020 will likely go down as a watershed for both our society and education. But we will likely not appreciate or recognize these changes for several years to come. It will likely change how we interact,

> It will likely change how we interact, where we live and work, whether we physically move for employment, and it will change the way or ways we learn.

where we live and work, whether we physically move for employment, and it will change the way or ways we learn.

After experiencing self-directed learning, project-based learning, hybrid learning, greater learner autonomy, and greater flexibility in general, many students are going to want and expect similar styles moving forward. Perhaps it has unfortunately taken a global pandemic for education to realize that it must move quickly to become more personalized, flexible, and learner-centric. These are not new concepts, nor are they new methods. They have been put into practice by many schools around the globe but have yet to become mainstream across the majority of schools, as our sector-wide infatuation with *What* overrides our need to focus on *Who*.

There are changes to education that are being solidified by the pandemic. Methods that have proven effective, even in the face of a crisis. These also, and not uncoincidentally, are areas that refocus attention on students' needs, interests, and agency – or personalization for short. These include the development and rise of:

◆ Learning communities
◆ Student agency
◆ Guide on the Side (as opposed to Sage on the Stage)
◆ Learning to Learn.[6]

Over this traumatic upending period, we have witnessed some schools succeed – they have thrived more than they have survived. These are the schools that have preemptively put in place some of the things we have been discussing and advocating for many years, not because of an impending pandemic but because it's good pedagogy.

The most successful schools and classrooms dealing with this crisis have been the ones that have developed a sense of student agency and ownership over their own learning. Trying to replicate a standard, traditional classroom where the teacher is constantly present does not work as we teach and learn remotely. Students needs to develop an understanding of their own role in the learning process and be expected and encouraged to see themselves more as agents, or ideally owners, of their own learning. For such ownership and agency to be developed students will need to assume greater responsibility, understand new expectations, and be introduced to this new or growing role in stages. Taking ownership, and agency, should be seen by both teachers and learners to be a process, and not the flicking of a switch.

Slade (2020)[7]

Hopefully we will use this experience to better understand the needs of our students and start to allow them to also better understand *Who* they are and could become.

From Voice and Agency to Ownership and Belonging

In a recent publication, *The Learning Compact Renewed: Whole Child for the Whole World* (ASCD, 2020),[8] Russell Quaglia, the executive director of the Quaglia Institute for School Voice and Aspirations, and Peter DeWitt, the author and speaker, outlined how:

> Student empowerment is fostered when school leaders and teachers create a school climate that values student voice.
>
> This collective empowerment of student voice comes to fruition and thrives when students can share their genuine thoughts, ideas, beliefs, and opinions, and contribute realistic solutions for the good of the whole, in an environment built on trust and respect and where students demonstrate a willingness and ability to listen and learn from others. Perhaps most important, student voice includes students being responsible for both what they say and

what they do. This responsibility encompasses taking action to make a difference beyond oneself.[9]

Student voice and agency do not only lead to improved learning but also grow the individual's sense of belonging. They become more responsible for their learning and become more engaged in the learning community.

> Somewhat ironically, the more we focus on the individual's learning styles and provide greater avenues for choice in learning, the more we develop the sense that we are all learning together.

Somewhat ironically, the more we focus on the individual's learning styles and provide greater avenues for choice in learning, the more we develop the sense that we are all learning together. Learning, as a function, becomes a team activity or a learning community.

When we seek to actively involve the students in the co-creation of learning with their teachers, and with the processes of the broader school in general, we discover that school becomes a learning ecosystem, a place where everyone is part of the learning process.

> School moves from being a place of sit-and-get and moves towards being a place of true collaboration. The culture of the school changes to be one about ownership, and co-creation, of learning.

School moves from being a place of sit-and-get and moves towards being a place of true collaboration. The culture of the school changes to be one about ownership, and co-creation, of learning.

[W]hen there are opportunities for the adults as well as the students to express their voice, co-create and design, recognize the significance of socially constructing learning, and discovering who they are as learners, a beautiful culture of interdependence in thinking flourished.

Zmuda & Kallick (2018)[10]

As we move along this continuum from standardization to personalization, from didactic learning to decision making and co-creation, we see the rise in student voice and student agency. Students, the learners themselves, expect and are expected to become more active agents in their own learning. This path becomes a virtuous circle where students – given more voice and agency – start to expect more voice and agency. The practice of ownership begets the desire and need for more ownership.

At its minimum, voice and choice shows up via student selection of topics or projects. While a positive step, this example keeps the onus for *What* is being taught and in what context firmly in the hands (and voice) of the teacher. The continuum of voice and choice extends, towards its other extreme, to where students themselves are deciding, with guidance from the teacher, on *What* is to be learned, *How*, and *Why*. Students, in understanding their own strengths and learning styles, are then best able to make decisions about how they learn best or what areas they wish to build on. They are also able to decide how mastery or understanding could best be demonstrated. This continuum could in fact extend all the way to where the learner is deciding, learning, and mastering without the help of the teacher having learned the skills of learning themselves. And isn't this an objective of lifelong learning itself, to develop learners who can learn throughout their lifetime? Are we not aiming as one of our core objectives to help develop such learners who can consciously and purposefully move along this continuum and become independent learners?

Raising and curating student voice taps into a myriad of additional skills and traits. It, of course, raises the students' voice and their independence. But in doing so it also requires them to foster and grow the skills of communication, deliberation, decision making, planning, and action. They become owners of their own learning (*step-by-step*) as we the educators (*step-by-step*) descend from that sage on the stage.

They become owners of their own learning (*step-by-step*) as we the educators (*step-by-step*) descend from that sage on the stage.

Inquiry, Exploration, and Discovery

We are seeing a pedagogical move from choice to voice; from action to agency. By developing an understanding of who they are, the learner at the same time is developing their skills of agency. Skills (*How*) are being learned in direct relationship to learning *Who* the learner is.

Inquiry-based learning is a form of learning where the learner is actively engaged in and seeking answers to questions that they have helped form. Start with a problem, then begin to plan and trial how to solve that problem. The starting point isn't a predetermined task or unit but rather a question to be answered, or an issue to be solved.

Conversely, traditional education would begin with presenting a series of facts or content to be learned that already solve a problem. Traditional education assumes that the answers have been discovered and the next course is to learn them. Inquiry-based education assumes that answers are there to be discovered, and the best answer may not yet have been found.

> Inquiry-based education assumes that answers are there to be discovered, and the best answer may not yet have been found.

Inquiry-based learning however does not mean that facts or content cannot be learned – as they are evidence of learning in their own right – but it places this learning in the context of inquiry. What have others discovered previously? How will this help or hinder what I'm now trying to solve?

It arose initially in the 1960s, during a time when much of education was focused around memorization and rote learning. Taking its cues from the works of John Dewey, Jean Piaget, and Lev Vygotsky, inquiry-based learning saw learning and inquiry as intertwined and also fundamental to the human condition. We are inquisitive and we want to learn, and the best pedagogy is one that plays to this natural instinct.

Inquiry-based learning in the next 50 years has expanded to include problem-based learning, experiential learning, exploratory learning, discovery learning, and design thinking, all of which take an initial question or query as the starting point. It also aligns with constructivist theory as it requires the learner to make meaning of the learning based on their personal or societal experience.

Inquiry-based learning can be extended further into what is known as exploratory learning. Here the teacher creates and curates situations and scenarios where the learner is actively exploring the situation, or in most cases the physical environment. Their current abilities can be matched with varying degrees of difficulty or complexity as they navigate through a learning experience or environment. Again, this method or approach attaches itself to the innate curiosity, or inquisitiveness, of the learner, as a core foundation and fundamental driver. The educator finds or establishes environments which compel the learner to explore and discover.

> The educator finds or establishes environments which compel the learner to explore and discover.

We see this in its simplest form in the development of playground equipment in preschools where each piece of equipment is designed to allow the learner to explore, discover, and experience challenges that help them understand about both themselves (what can I do) and their world (if I lean backwards this moves). The monkey-bars and see-saws of many of our childhoods also did this but the sheer creativity and design thinking that goes into playground equipment nowadays allows children to learn about movement, weight, gravity, momentum, centrifugal force, and balance years before they will ever need to know the words.

> . . . allows children to learn about movement, weight, gravity, momentum, centrifugal force, and balance years before they will ever need to know the words.

It is learning through action; learning through exploration.

Another great example is from an East Bay elementary school in the San Francisco Bay area. They were studying fossils and rather than learn from texts, the teachers would take their fossil models to the Alameda foreshore the night before and bury them in the sand. The next day during a regular field trip, the students would be sent out to 're-discover' the fossils in a similar manner to how they would be discovered by archeologists. Time consuming on the part of the teachers – yes, but time worth spent in learning by the students – definitely.

In these situations, the learning and discovery is owned by the learner. They are the ones wanting to discover because the learning environments are compelling. They move through the experience at their own pace, discovering as they go. It also means that the teachers' work is mainly done at the start or before the activity, in preparing the learning environment. As such, the teacher can watch the learning take place, evaluate what is working and what is not in real time, and adjust or curate changes for the next time, or for the next experience.

Such experiences are enhanced by discussing with the students what they learned, how they learned it, what they are still not understanding, or still wish to learn. Such debriefs or feedback sessions allow the students to be more aware of what they are doing naturally – discovering and learning.

The concept has been taken to even greater extremes by museums and exhibition halls. The Exploratorium in San Francisco, first opened in 1969 and created by Frank Oppenheimer (yes, that one), transformed the empty Palace of Fine Arts into a science learning experience. Over the next 50-plus years it has grown, and moved, to become one of the best examples of an immersive active learning experience. A plywood sign from a workshop declares "Here is being created the Exploratorium, a community museum dedicated to awareness."

> Our mission is to create inquiry-based experiences that transform learning worldwide. Our vision is a world where people think for themselves and can confidently ask questions, question answers, and understand the world around them. We value lifelong learning and teaching, curiosity and inquiry, our community, iteration and evidence, integrity and authenticity, sustainability, and inclusion and respect. We create tools and experiences that help you to become an active explorer.
> Exploratorium: The Museum of Science,
> Art and Human Perception[11]

Want true discovery in an unpredictable (or less predictable) setting? Outdoor education has taken self-discovery and discovery learning to a new level. Immerse the learner in what is typically for them a new and uncertain environment, and let the discovery begin.

Immerse the learner in what is typically for them a new and uncertain environment, and let the discovery begin.

Of course, the experiences are much more deliberate and defined than that, but for many who experience outdoor education that is how it feels. And that is half the point – to take you out of your comfort zone and have you experience new activities or solve new problems surrounded by uncertainty.

Outdoor education prides itself on establishing the perception of high risk in a setting of actual low risk. The learner is confronting their fears or apprehensions, as well as their physical ability to complete an activity, and in well-designed experiences they are able to adjust, adapt, and succeed in mastering that activity. It not only allows them to learn, trial, and adjust what they are doing in real time, it is also pushing their ability to confront challenges and make decisions. Take a ropes course where the learner feels unsafe and unsure – as they've likely never experienced this activity before – but in fact they are roped in, attached, and guided every step of the way. The same applies during rock climbing or abseiling: the fear and apprehension the learner experiences as they lean backwards over the edge of the cliff, their support, and trust only being held by the supporting tether.

> Risk plays about as pivotal role in experiential education as oxygen does in sustaining the human body… risk taking is not only critical to the learning process but it is also essential to the maintenance of the human spirit.
>
> Liddle (1998)[12]

What these activities do is change one's self-perception of what we are capable of and in doing so who we are. They change our self-efficacy and shape our undertaking of ourselves.

They change our self-efficacy and shape our understanding of ourselves.

Outward Bound, one of the first and most prominent actors in delivering outdoor education experience, has had great success in transforming the lives of many at-risk youth. It impacts perceptions of personal empowerment[13] and can have a lasting impact on both the self-esteem and self-efficacy of youth, which can transfer into other parts of their lives both in and out of school.[14] It helps us understand more of who we are, and who we can be.

These lessons appear to be long-lasting. Research conducted by the famed researcher John Hattie early in his career – 'Adventure Education and Outward Bound: Out-of-Class Experiences That Make a Lasting Difference' – found that: "In a remarkable contrast to most educational research, these short-term or immediate gains were followed by substantial additional gains between the end of the program and follow-up assessments... and improved as the length of the program and the ages of participants increased."[15]

And research has also found that Outward Bound also increases one's likelihood of engaging in public and civic service. A study conducted by Bolick and Nilsen ('Outward Bound and Civic-Minded: The Impact of an Outward Bound Course on Students' Understanding of and Experiences with Public Service') found a clear relationship between an outdoor education experience and public service.[16]

> It can also help us apparently understand who 'we' (*plural*) are.

It can also help us apparently understand who the 'we' (*plural*) are. In this vein of self-discovery and civic engagement, Outward Bound is currently extending a partnership with the Ministry of Education in Singapore – coincidentally one of the leading countries in education globally according to the OECD's Programme for International Student Assessment (PISA) – to develop and roll out a nationwide Outward Bound program for all youth. Why? "[T]o prepare the next generation for the challenges of an increasingly uncertain and volatile world by developing critical life skills."[17] The benefit of such experiences, as was stated by PM Lee Hsien Loong at the 50th Anniversary Celebrations for Outward Bound Singapore (OBS), in a speech delivered on November 29, 2017, is to "ignite the excitement of the trainees, stretch their limits and encourage their self-discovery, while letting them test and push boundaries in a safe and nurturing environment."[18]

It is about discovering who we are, who we can be, and not limiting ourselves to preconceived ideas of ourselves that have not yet been pushed or challenged.

As Kurt Hahn, Outward Bound founder, stated: "There is more to us than we know. If we can be made to see it, perhaps for the rest of our lives we will be unwilling to settle for less."[19]

The Collective Who

Dr. Philip Rodkin, the late Associate Professor at the University of Illinois, would often talk about classrooms as being *communities of thirty*.[20] *Communities of thirty* where students are able, and frequently required, to learn not only cognitively, but also socially and emotionally. In this mini-community, students learn and practice how to interact with others on a daily basis. They learn how to disagree, dispute, debate, how to form a consensus, and how to work with others. They also learn how to make this community – this learning environment – a successful, productive, and inclusive environment. They learn how to work together as a group, a team, and as a community.

> They also learn how to make this community – this learning environment – a successful, productive, and inclusive environment. They learn how to work together as a group, a team, and as a community.

What is occurring here, as the students learn and interact, is the development of a sense of belonging and a communal set of values, expectations, and norms. These may be similar to other norms in other classrooms, or they may be slightly different as they are made by the members of the classroom community themselves.

Just as each classroom and each school develops its own norms, so do our larger communities and our societies. These are the plural 'who' that make up who we all are.

Schools that promote and develop citizenship norms – democracy, voting, opinions – are influencing what is important in the community. These traits become normalized and students become more aware, and skilled at them, and expect these across their communities. The same can be seen in the progression for more inclusive communities and societies. Public schools, formed on the premise of equality and fairness, can often be the first entre into equality in a community. When the underlying premise is equitable opportunity in learning, it is difficult, though not impossible, to ignore or sideline a subsection of that school.

> Schools are both a mirror of our communities and an influence on their progress.

Schools are both a mirror of our communities and an influence on their progress. As we embark on more personalized learning, with a focus on the individual developing how and where they can make their education meaningful, we will continue to see the effect extend into and across our communities.

Horace Mann, the founder of the first Common School and as such founder of what we now call our Public School system, declared that education, "beyond all other devices of human origin, is a great equalizer of the conditions of men—the balance wheel of the social machinery."[21] He set forth a premise that we hold onto today that education can and does change individual lives and, as a product of its process, changes our communities as well.

> A State should... seek the solution of such problems as these. To what extent can competence [knowledge] displace pauperism [poverty]? How nearly can we free ourselves from the low-minded and the vicious, not by their expatriation [removal] but by their elevation? To what extent can the resources and powers of Nature be converted into human welfare, the peaceful arts of life be advanced and the vast treasures of human talent and genius be developed? How much of suffering, in all its forms, can be relieved? Or, what is better than relief; how much can be prevented? Cannot the classes of crimes be lessened, and the number of criminals in each class be diminished? ... The distance between the two extremes of society is lengthening, instead of being abridged. With every generation, fortunes increase on the one hand. And some new privation is added to poverty on the other. We are verging towards those extremes of opulence [wealth] and of penny [poverty], each of which unhumanizes the mind...
>
> ...it would do more than all things else to obliterate [erase] distinctions in society. But the beneficient [helpful] power of education would not be exhausted, even though it should peaceably abolish all the miseries that spring from co-existence, side by side, of enormous wealth and squalid want. It has a higher function. Beyond the power of

diffusing old wealth, it has the prerogative [power] of creating new. It is a thousand times more lucrative [profitable] than fraud, and adds a thousand fold more to a nation's resources than the most successful conquests. Knaves and robbers can obtain only what was before possessed by others. But education creates or develops new treasures, treasures not before possessed or dreamed of by anyone.

Mann (1848)[22]

Education plays a role in determining who we are, and who we want to be, as a society. Whether it has been the anti-Vietnam protests at Kent State University, and the subsequent student strike of some four-million students across the US in 1970, which stemmed directly from the killing of four protesters by the Ohio National Guard, or the earlier protests, riots, and battles over school integration in the 1950s, education and its schools and students have played a major role in moving society forward.

> Education plays a role in determining who we are, and who we want to be, as a society.

What occurred in 1957 at Little Rock Central High School in Arkansas, as the first real test of the passing of *Brown v. Board of Education* some three years earlier, drew a nationwide discussion regarding what is and isn't considered acceptable in our society. Though large parts of the country persisted through the decade in refusing to make schools accessible to all students regardless of color, this now appears abnormal, inhumane, and overtly unjust. The actions of the nine students in 1957 helped start a societal debate on who we are, and while these changes take time, there is a general realization that the stance or opinions of one generation are often changed by the deliberations and discussions of the next. Whether it is the debate and discussion of societal issues, the development of opinion, or the mere fact that schools and universities are inhabited by the next generation, education has and continues to play a major role in advancing social change.

One should never forget the immense moral pressure of such a great judgment as that just announced, and its capacity to persuade men of good will who have been doubting and hesitating. No state in the Union is populated by a separate species of cruel and brutal white men, seeking by cynical devices or by sheer defiance to escape the performance of constitutional duties. One has only to travel in the present South to realize the contrary—to be convinced of the rapid increase of humanitarianism, of cultivation, of kindness, of comfort, of all the good things that go to make up a great civilization.

Sutherland (1954)[23]

In more recent years with more focused attention directed towards inclusion and equity, we have seen changes to societal expectations around disabilities, gender and gender identification, and basic rights.

Education has led the way more often than not in increasing equity in and across our society, putting into practice the ideals and declarations that we wish to see to make

> Education has led the way more often than not in increasing equity in and across our society . . .

our society more equitable and more aligned with our theoretical assumptions of who 'we' (plural) want to be – whether that be *Brown v Board of Education*, affirmative action, the school lunch program, or disability rights.

UNICEF has called "Disability… the single most serious barrier to education across the globe."[24] By ignoring, not confronting, or pushing this issue to the side, we alienate a broad section of our population and push them to the periphery of our society where they may be catered for, but too often not educated. We cast their destiny without them having a say or a voice in it.

Curt Dudley-Marling and Mary Bridget Burns, both of Boston College at the time of their article, 'Two Perspectives on Inclusion in the United States,' give a concise overview of the exclusionary policies and tactics that condemned students with disabilities to a restricted education and a subsequent restrictive life in society. Many students with disabilities, prior to the passing of the *Education for All Handicapped Children Act* in 1975, were denied free public education, and those that were permitted to attend public school were at best ill-served and forced to endure restrictions inside the school itself. The concept of inclusive classrooms that we enjoy today was a rarity that few benefited from.

> Prior to the enactment of the landmark Education for All Children Act (also known as Public Law 94–142), only one in five students with disabilities in the US were educated in public schools. Moreover, many states had laws on their books that explicitly excluded many students with disabilities from public schooling including children who had been labeled deaf, blind, emotionally disturbed.
>
> Dudley-Marling & Burns (2014)[25]

For many states, students with disabilities were considered uneducable. Accommodations weren't really accommodations but rather formal ways to keep students with disabilities away from the traditional school system.

> In his *History of Inclusion in the United States*, Robert Osgood (2005) observed that, until relatively recently, a significant proportion of students with disabilities in the US, especially students with intellectual disabilities, were considered uneducable. These students were completely excluded from public schooling. Even those students with disabilities who were considered to be "educable" were typically segregated within schools since it was presumed that these students had unique educational needs requiring the services of specially trained professionals.
>
> Ibid.

Many educators also resisted inclusion as their training and more rigid teaching methodologies didn't cater to individual needs. Adjustments to learning styles were rare and adjustment to a disability rarer still.

Since the passing of the *Education for All Handicapped Children Act*,[26] progress has been constant but it has taken a while to get to where we are today, both as a society and a system of schools.

In 1990 the act was renamed the *Individuals with Disabilities Education Act* (IDEA) and has passed a series of updates, improvements, and clarifications to get us to where we are today.

Today in the US, schools must provide students with disabilities "free appropriate public education that is tailored to their individual needs; and wherever possible students should have the same accommodations to learning as any other student receives."[27] The act has at its core a premise of equity and inclusion, and as such, students, both those with and without disabilities, have been shown to benefit from such approaches.

It is, of course, not surprising to find that students with disabilities benefit from inclusion. These are not only academic benefits[28] but also, and perhaps equally as importantly, research has found improvements in sense of belonging, cohesion,[29] and as a result, attendance.[30] These are all common-sense and expected outcomes.

When people feel part of a group and accepted, they will likely want to remain part of that setting. Subsequently, students who feel like they belong attend school more often, and tend to also do better academically.

> When people feel part of a group and accepted, they will likely want to remain part of that setting.

But what is also interesting is that the fears that many parents and politicians felt in 1975 – that inclusion would water down or harm the learning of students without disabilities – have been debunked. Studies have found that there is either no change or in fact improvement in academics.[31] Perhaps more importantly, inclusion has given rise to broader acceptance of inclusion and equity across the school system and into society.

As Dr. Thomas Hehir highlighted in 'A Summary of the Evidence on Inclusive Education':

Attending class alongside a student with a disability can yield positive impacts on the social attitudes and beliefs of non-disabled students... [these include] reduced fear of human differences, accompanied by increased comfort and awareness (less fear of people who look or behave differently); growth in social cognition (increased tolerance of others, more effective communication with all peers); improvements in self-concept (increased self-esteem, perceived status, and sense of belonging); development of personal moral and ethical principles (less prejudice, higher responsiveness to the needs of others); and warm and caring friendships.

Hehir (2016)[32]

At this point let's take a step back to ask ourselves *Why* we have an education system and *Who* we want to be as a society:

◆ Reduced fear of human differences, accompanied by increased comfort and awareness
◆ Growth in social cognition
◆ Improvements in self-concept
◆ Development of personal moral and ethical principles
◆ Warm and caring friendships.

Inclusive schools and classrooms are able to actively develop many of the skills, attitudes, and attributes we want to see in our society.

◆ Empathy
◆ Belonging
◆ Reduction in prejudice
◆ Increase in sense of community
◆ Improved self-concept.

This infusion of inclusion has gone hand in hand with other educational approaches in the US and many other countries.

> As the movement towards personalization of learning has increased so has the movement for inclusion.

As the movement towards personalization of learning has increased so has the movement for inclusion. The basic premise is that if we can personalize for one non-disabled student then surely we can (and should ethically) accommodate for every student.

Schools now offer Individual Education Plans, or IEPs, to suit the needs of a myriad of learning styles. These plans are able to provide specific context and individualized instructional plans for students who may need a different approach or accommodation spanning autism, deaf-blindness, deafness, developmental delay, emotional disturbance, hearing impairment, intellectual disability, multiple disabilities, orthopedic impairment, other health impairment, specific learning disability, speech impairment, traumatic brain injury, and visual impairment.

Those involved in education over the past decade won't be surprised to hear that educators in Finland have taken this concept of IEPs even further mainstream. While some 14% of students in the US may receive IEPs, or special education services, in Finland it's over 30% with many students utilizing services for a short period of time or as needed. Schools are well funded and supported to provide these services.

> I recently visited the Hiidenkivi Comprehensive School in Helsinki, Finland, to see how the educators provide special education. It is a typical suburban public school that serves 760 students in grades 1–9. More than 10 percent are from immigrant-background homes.
>
> Three special education classes of eight students each were led by a special education teacher and supported by one or two trained assistants. Thirty-nine other students with varying special needs were integrated into regular classes with the help of an expert teacher. The teachers and administrators had designed a curriculum that suggests this school invests heavily in ensuring all students have access to effective instruction and individualized help.
>
> Sahlberg (2012)[33]

And one other small but significant difference? In Finland the term used isn't 'Special Education' but a more generic 'Learning and Schooling Support.'

In Finland the term used isn't 'Special Education' but a more generic 'Learning and Schooling Support.'

First, in Finland, special education is defined primarily as addressing learning difficulties in reading, writing, mathematics or foreign languages. In the United States and in many other nations, students are identified as having special education needs if they meet criteria for a variety of disabling conditions such as sensory and speech-language impairments, intellectual disabilities and behavioral problems.

Second, in Finland, special education needs are identified early, and prevention is a common strategy. As a result, a larger percentage of children are identified as special-education students in Finland than in the United States. In Finnish comprehensive schools (corresponding to K-9 education in the United States), almost one-third of all pupils are in part- or full-time special education.

Finally, Finnish special education is called learning and schooling support and encompasses three categories of support for those students with special needs: general support, intensified support and special support.

General support includes actions by the regular classroom teacher in terms of differentiation, as well as efforts by the school to cope with student diversity. Intensified support consists of remedial support by the teacher, co-teaching with the special education teacher, and individual or small-group learning with a part-time special education teacher. Special support includes a wide range of special-education services, from full-time general education to placement in a special institution. All students in this category are assigned an individual learning plan.

Ibid.[34]

Who Do We Collectively Want to Be?

When 15-year-old student Gavin Grimm came out as trans-gender, his school principal gave him permission to use the boys' bathroom. For two months this continued without issues among his classmates, teachers, and administrators. However, as a result of parent complaints his school, Gloucester County High School in Virginia, officially banned him from using the boys' bathroom in December 2014. That ban included not only bathroom use but also locker rooms and would affect and impact any other trans-gender students. The American Civil Liberties Union (ACLU) took up Gavin's – and all other transgender students' rights – and a suit was filed on June 11, 2015 against the Gloucester County School Board. The complaint, filed with the U.S. Department of Justice, claimed that the policy violates Gavin's rights under federal laws that prohibit sex discrimination in public schools that receive federal funds. The case eventually went all the way to the Supreme Court where, on August 26, 2020, Gavin was victorious. This was a victory not only for Gavin but for transgender students across the country.

Between 2014 and 2020, public support for the rights of transgender students grew, with leaders across federal and state government aligning their support with Gavin and four other Virginian district school boards – Fairfax County, Arlington County, Falls Church, and Alexandria City – filing briefs in support of Gavin Grimm and his case. The case, stemming from a school, brought a national discussion on who we are and who we want to be as a nation and a society to the fore.

> . . . a national discussion on who we are and who we want to be as a nation and a society . . .

This has not been without struggle nor controversy. Many states reacted and counteracted by passing anti-transgender bills, particularly in more conservative regions, but at the same time Gay–Straight Alliances and support for LGBTQ+ students have continued to grow.

According to the *Gay–Straight Alliance Network*, a San Francisco advocacy organization founded in 1998, which has formally changed its name to *Genders & Sexualities Alliance Network*, there are now more than 4,000 Gay–Straight Alliance or Genders and Sexualities Alliance (GSA) clubs across the nation, being represented by a network of 40 statewide organizations.[35] GSAs have grown in number since the original club was formed in November 1988 at Concord Academy in Concord, Massachusetts. In that instance it was Kevin Jennings, a history teacher at the school who had just come out as gay, and would later become the Assistant Deputy Secretary of Education for the Office of Safe and Drug-Free Schools with the US Department of Education, who was approached by Meredith Sterling, a student who was upset by the treatment of gay students. Together, Jennings and Sterling were able to recruit other supportive staff and students to form the first Gay–Straight alliance.

From this small start, GSAs have grown to be commonplace in the majority of states and districts nationally. According to the US Centers for Disease Control and Prevention's (CDC) School Health Profiles, a system of surveys assessing school health policies and practices in states, large urban school districts, and territories, 40% of schools now have a GSA, which is a rise of 73% since 2008. These numbers vary by state, from a high of between 50 and 74% across California, Delaware, Florida, Maine, Massachusetts, New York, Rhode Island, Vermont, and Washington, to a low of 0–24% in Alaska, Arkansas, Mississippi, Montana, Nebraska, Oklahoma, South Dakota, and Tennessee.[36] But the continued growth shows that public opinion is changing and that schools are mirroring, if not forecasting, these changes. This rise in support of equality and support of developing safe and supportive environments for all students regardless of gender preference or identification matches the rise in public support of other changes in society. There is no causal data to indicate or suggest that changes in attitudes in our youth lead to direct changes in our societies but there is correlational data. Support for LGBTQ+ students has been increasing consistently and at a rapid rate since the first GSA was formed in 1989.

From 1996 to 2020, public support for gay marriage in the US has grown exponentially. It has basically flipped from two-thirds disapproving towards the end of the last century to two-thirds approving as of 2020.[37] In the space of just over two decades, it has undertaken what Malcolm Gladwell might call a tipping point and tipped.

In the space of just over two decades, it has undertaken what Malcolm Gladwell[38] might call a tipping point and tipped.

Along with the support for same-sex marriage there have been other adjacent equality-focused changes that have played out in the military and society writ large. These include the 1994 'Don't Ask, Don't Tell' (DADT) legislation, which was originally put in place as a way to adjust or attempt to accommodate military service by gay men, bisexuals, and lesbians. This was repealed in 2011 as it was viewed by both the public and the military as discriminatory and counterproductive. The military now has no restrictions on LGBTQ+ service. When DADT was instituted, public support for gay and lesbian service was at 44%.[39] When it was repealed in 2011, public support had grown to 77%.[40]

Changes in our society are reflected in our schools, yet often changes in our schools preempt changes in our broader society. Why is that? Primarily because our schools are based on providing the best opportunity for each student to learn.

. . . our schools are based on providing the best opportunity for each student to learn.

To accommodate individual differences and needs, adjustments are made to allow that child to thrive. A child's ability to get to and attend school, to see the whiteboard, to not be bullied, should not impact their opportunity and ability to learn. Accommodations are made and adjustments put in place to suit the needs of the learner. A child's gender, preferred pronoun, race, religion, or culture should not provide them with less opportunity. Policies are developed and processes are modified or recreated. Such changes in the education setting become established primarily out of a desire to ensure equitable learning environments where each student has the same opportunities and access to supports. However, there is another function at play.

As we seek to develop students' ability to think critically and creatively, problem solve, and develop empathy – what many have termed 21st century learning skills – they are discussing and debating current issues and debating them for clarity and understanding. This isn't anything new to be honest as many generations of students have been debating issues for many decades or rather centuries, but what is different now is that we understand that these skills are more needed, desired, and essential.

> Aligned to our need to promote equitable learning environments is the need to develop the skills that our students will require this century.

Aligned to our need to promote equitable learning environments is the need to develop the skills that our students will require this century. Coincidentally, these two areas also align with our call to better understand who we are and who we want to be.

Peter DeWitt, the author and speaker, hypothesized on this in his *EdWeek* article 'Adults Are Banning Classroom Topics. Perhaps They Should Allow Students to Explore Them?':

> School is supposed to be a venue where students have numerous opportunities to engage in deep learning that will prepare them for their future. That learning is supposed to foster the ability for students to engage in their own learning around topics that they care about and perhaps even want to pursue after they leave high school and enter career and technical education, higher education, or the workforce in an internship capacity.
>
> As teachers, we need to be allowed to explore issues with students like mathematical concepts, scientific problems that need our greatest thinking, or societal problems that need to be resolved. After all, we are supposed to empower students to feel they can change the world and not enable them to feel they can't do anything to change it at all.
>
> DeWitt (2021)[41]

However, as with much in society, change is often not linear nor easy. While public opinion has shifted and grown in support of transgender rights, many of the earlier policies enacted during the Obama administration were rolled back at both the federal and state level during the Trump administration. Early signs in the Biden administration indicate that many of the changes to policy enacted by President Obama to support transgender students and adults will be reenacted and likely increased. The education secretary has declared that "the Department makes clear that all students—including LGBTQ+ students—deserve the opportunity to learn and thrive in schools that are free from discrimination," putting into educational systems practice what has already been passed by the Supreme Court.

> The Supreme Court has upheld the right for LGBTQ+ people to live and work without fear of harassment, exclusion, and discrimination—and our LGBTQ+ students have the same rights and deserve the same protections. I'm proud to have directed the Office for Civil Rights to enforce Title IX to protect all students from all forms of sex discrimination.
>
> U.S. Department of Education Press Release (2021)[42]

There is a continuous evolution of our communities and society. It does not always stem from the classroom, but it is often reinforced or discussed in the classroom. Societal norms have a myriad of influences and influencers from national events, protests, and political events, to pop culture, literature, and media. This is an ongoing push me–pull me sequence of inputs, discussions, and events, that form our identity, as an individual, a community, and a society. But to dismiss the school or classroom as a place where this identity is, or can be, fostered would be folly. Our collective identities – our who – are being formed by all of us and are being formed by those of the next generation who will inherit or claim power, position, and voice.

Our collective identities – our who – are being formed by all of us and are being formed by those of the next generation who will inherit or claim power, position, and voice.

A broad and expansive example of this is the infusion of the UN's Sustainable Development Goals (SDGs) into K12 activities. In 2015 the United Nations ratified the SDGs, 17 goals that range from the environment, to education, to transportation, which nations have signed up to achieve with a target date of 2030. School systems around the world have been encouraged to align these goals and their desired outcomes into relevant and aligned subject areas. UNESCO has developed a series of lesson plans and activities to help infuse Education for Sustainable Development (ESD), a key theme across all SDGs, into any K12 setting. Teaching colleges around the US have also developed units to focus on the goals and their relevance to education. Probably the largest and most widespread example of the infusion of the SDGs into lessons is Project Everyone's 'World's Largest Lesson' initiative that promotes the "use of the Sustainable Development Goals in learning so that children can contribute to a better future for all. From citizenship and justice to climate change and the environment, inspire children to make a difference!"[43]

As of 2019 they had already reached 17.9 million children located in over 160 countries. The World's Largest Lesson believes that by promoting the use of the SDGs in learning, "we can help show students that a better world is possible" and that "children can contribute to a better future for all."

A more direct and obvious example of this is the work undertaken by two school-age girls whose actions raised their own questioning of who we are, and who we want to be – Greta and Malala.

Malala Yousafzai in 2012 spoke out publicly on behalf of girls and their right to learn in her native Pakistan. As a consequence, she was targeted and shot by those opposing both her outspokenness and her call for girls' education. Her continued campaigning and determination to change what she wants to see in schools and across society has already borne success. She has more than anyone else raised the issue globally, winning the Nobel Peace Prize in 2014 and becoming the youngest ever Nobel laureate, establishing a fund worth $22 million and now spanning projects active in eight countries from Afghanistan to Nigeria to Brazil. More than that, she has changed the national dialogue in many countries about how we are treating our girls.

> . . . she has changed the national dialogue in many countries about how we are treating our girls.

Greta Thunberg, who in 2018 began skipping school to camp out in front of the Swedish Parliament to protest about the lack of deliberate action being taken to confront climate change, has similarly launched a global dialogue around a core issue based on who we are as a society. Do we want to be the generation that ignored the science and turned away to do nothing? Or do we want to be the generation – and society – that rallies for each other and our planet?

Both Malala and Greta have become leaders in confronting the status quo, and in asking who are we? And in doing so they not only spark change, but also spark more questioning of ourselves.

Along the way, she [Greta] emerged as a standard bearer in a generational battle, an avatar of youth activists across the globe fighting for everything from gun control to democratic representation. Her global climate strike is the largest and most international of all the youth movements, but it's hardly the only one: teenagers in the U.S. are organizing against gun violence and flocking to progressive candidates; students in Hong Kong are battling for democratic representation; and young people from South America to Europe are agitating for remaking the global economy. Thunberg is not aligned with these disparate protests, but her insistent presence has come to represent the fury of youth worldwide.

TIME Magazine (2019)[44]

These are the broadest of *Who*'s – not just the school or community but the role we play in helping our world. *Who* do we want to be as a society? What world do we want to live in? And what role do our students themselves – our children and youth – play in determining this future?

Who do we want to be as a society? What world do we want to live in? And what role do our students themselves – our children and youth – play in determining this future?

Who in the Classroom

Questions to ask yourself

- ◆ How have my experiences in and out of school changed or affected who I am?
- ◆ What experiences do I want to craft to allow my students to learn who they are?
- ◆ Does how I teach authentically reflect who I am?

Questions to ask your students

- ◆ What did you discover about yourself during that last [topic/unit/activity]?
- ◆ Was there anything that surprised you?
- ◆ How has your understanding of yourself changed over the last year?
- ◆ Is there anything about what you discovered that you can use in other parts of your life?

Questions for your students to ask themselves

- ◆ This is as much about determining who we are {plural} as it is about discovering who we each are {singular}. Who do you want us to be or become?
- ◆ What role can you play in helping us get there?

Notes

1   Montessori, M. & Claremont, *The Absorbent Mind*, Dell Pub. Co., 1969, p. 257.
2   Hoerr, T., *Fostering Grit: How Do I Prepare My Students for the Real World?*, ASCD, 2013.
3   Buckley, D., 'Personalisation: The SECRET of Success,' 2005. https://slideplayer.com/slide/13746791/
4   Spencer. G., 'Schools after COVID-19: From a Teaching Culture to a Learning Culture,' June 17, 2020. https://news.microsoft.com/apac/features/technology-in-schools-from-a-teaching-culture-to-a-learning-culture/

5   Spencer, G., Ibid.
6   Slade, S., 'How Covid-19 Will Force Education into the Future', ASCD Inservice, April 24, 2020. www.ascd.org/blogs/how-covid-19-will-force-education-into-the-future
7   Slade, S., Ibid.
8   *The Learning Compact Renewed – Whole Child for the Whole World*, ASCD, 2020.
9   *The Learning Compact Renewed*, Ibid.
10   Zmuda, A. & Kallick, B., 'Four Attributes to Grow a Personalized Learning Culture,' January 30, 2018. https://inservice.ascd.org/four-attributes-to-grow-a-personalized-learning-culture/
11   Exploratorium: The Museum of Science, Art and Human Perception, San Francisco. www.exploratorium.edu/
12   Liddle, J., 'Risk Management: Walking the Tightrope,' *Journal of Experiential Education*, Vol. 21, No. 2 (Sept.–Oct. 1998): 61.
13   Sibthorp, J., 'An Empirical Look at Walsh and Golins' Adventure Education Process Model: Relationships between Antecedent Factors, Perceptions of Characteristics of an Adventure Education Experience, and Changes in Self-Efficacy,' *Journal of Leisure Research*, Vol. 35, No. 1 (2003): 80–106.
14   Outward Bound Trust, 'New Research: Outdoor Learning and Self-efficacy,' May 23, 2017. www.schooltravelorganiser.com/features/new-research-outdoor-learning-and-self-efficacy/6618.article
15   Hattie, J., Marsh, J., & Richards, G., 'Adventure Education and Outward Bound: Out-of-Class Experiences That Make a Lasting Difference,' *Review of Educational Research*, Vol. 67, No. 1 (1997): 43–87. https://journals.sagepub.com/doi/10.3102/00346543067001043
16   Mason Bolick, C. & Nilsen, R., 'Outward Bound and Civic-Minded: The Impact of an Outward Bound Course on Students' Understanding of and Experiences with Public Service,' *Journal of Outdoor Recreation, Education, and Leadership*, Vol. 11, No. 2 (2019). https://js.sagamorepub.com/jorel/article/view/9264
17   'Stories of Impact,' *Outward Bound*. www.outwardbound.net/stories-of-impact/
18   'PM Lee Hsien Loong at OBS 50th Anniversary Celebrations,' 29 November 2017. www.pmo.gov.sg/Newsroom/pm-lee-hsien-loong-obs-50th-anniversary-celebrations

19   Kurt Hahn quote, *Outward Bound*. www.outwardbound.org/ about-outward-bound/outward-bound-today/history/

20   Slade, S., 'It's On Us', ASCD Inservice, November 26, 2016.

21   Mann, H., 'Report No. 12 of the Massachusetts School Board (1848).' https://usa.usembassy.de/etexts/democrac/16.htm

22   Mann, H., Ibid.

23   Sutherland, A.E., 'Segregation and the Supreme Court', *The Atlantic*, July 1954. www.theatlantic.com/magazine/archive/1954/07/ segregation-and-the-supreme-court/306055/

24   UNICEF, 'Inclusive Education – Every Child Has the Right to Quality Education and Learning.' www.unicef.org/education/ inclusive-education

25   Dudley-Marling, C. & Burns, M.B., 'Two Perspectives on Inclusion in the United States', Global Education Review, Vol. 1, No. 1 (2014): 14– 31 https://files.eric.ed.gov/fulltext/EJ1055208.pdf

26   Education for All Handicapped Children Act of 1975, www. govtrack.us/congress/bills/94/s6

27   Individuals with Disabilities Education Act, 20 U.S.C. § 1400 (2004).

28   Ford, J., 'Educating Students with Learning Disabilities in Inclusive Classrooms', *Electronic Journal for Inclusive Education*, Vol. 3, No. 4 (Summer/Fall 2015).

29   Rose, R. & Shevlin, M., 'A Sense of Belonging: Childrens' Views of Acceptance in "Inclusive" Mainstream Schools', *International Journal of Whole* Schooling, Vol. 13, No. 1 (Jan. 2017): 65–80.

30   Sakız, H., 'Impact of an Inclusive Programme on Achievement, Attendance and Perceptions Towards the School Climate and Social-Emotional Adaptation Among Students with Disabilities, *Educational Psychology*, Vol. 37, No. 5 (2017): 611–631. https://doi. org/10.1080/01443410.2016.1225001

31   Kalambouka, A., Farrell, P., Dyson, A., & Kaplan, I., 'The Impact of Placing Pupils with Special Educational Needs in Mainstream Schools on the Achievement of Their Peers', *Educational Research*, Vol. 49, No. 4 (Dec. 2007): 365–382. https://eric.ed.gov/?id= EJ779701

32   Hehir, T., *A Summary of the Evidence on Inclusive Education*, Alana, 2016. https://alana.org.br/wp-content/uploads/2016/12/A_Summary_ of_the_evidence_on_inclusive_education.pdf

33 Sahlberg, P., 'Quality and Equity in Finnish Schools,' *School Administrator* magazine, No. 8, Vol. 69 (Sept. 2012): 27–30. www. aasa.org/content.aspx?id=24592

34 Sahlberg, P., Ibid.

35 Gay Straight Alliance Network. https://gsanetwork.org/mission-vision-history/

36 Healthy People 2020, 'Adolescent Health, Objectives.' www. healthypeople.gov/2020/topics-objectives/topic/Adolescent-Health/objectives#3964

37 McCarthy, J., 'U.S. Support for Same-Sex Marriage Matches Record High', *Gallup News*, June 1, 2020. https://news.gallup.com/poll/311672/support-sex-marriage-matches-record-high.aspx

38 Gladwell, M., *The Tipping Point: How Little Things Can Make a Big Difference*, Wheeler Publishing, 2003.

39 McCarthy, J., 'U.S. Support for Same-Sex Marriage Matches Record High,' *Gallup News*, June 1, 2020. https://news.gallup.com/poll/311672/support-sex-marriage-matches-record-high.aspx

40 Thompson, M., 'Why Is the Military Polling the Troops about Gays?,' *TIME*, July 12, 2010. https://content.time.com/time/nation/article/0,8599,2003075,00.html

41 DeWitt, P., 'Adults Are Banning Classroom Topics. Perhaps They Should Allow Students to Explore Them?,' *EdWeek*, June 27, 2021. www.edweek.org/leadership/opinion-adults-are-banning-classroom-topics-perhaps-they-should-allow-students-to-explore-them/2021/06

42 U.S. Department of Education Press Release, 'U.S. Department of Education Confirms Title IX Protects Students from Discrimination Based on Sexual Orientation and Gender Identity,' June 16, 2021. www.ed.gov/news/press-releases/us-department-education-confirms-title-ix-protects-students-discrimination-based-sexual-orientation-and-gender-identity

43 World's Largest Lesson. https://worldslargestlesson.globalgoals.org/

44 *TIME Magazine*, 'TIME Person of the Year 2019 – Greta Thunberg.' https://time.com/person-of-the-year-2019-greta-thunberg/

6

Where and When

Where and *When* provide meaning and context. They place us, and our learning, on an axis of location and time. *Where* – this geographic location, whether it be our country, our state, or our town, suburb, and street – narrows what should be taught as learning should ultimately be meaningful and purposeful. Our other axis – *When* – focuses our attention on both issues that are current and also issues that have relevance from our past. We do not need to, nor could we, learn every current or historical act. We learn about certain changes to our previous thinking and understanding; actions which subsequently helped to create change; and the results, or lessons learned, from such changes. If we want to truly burrow down into *Why* we learn some of these historical occurrences, we should look no further than the previous chapter. We are learning about *Who* we are as a society and how that has come to be.

Current events and incidents allow us to both better understand our world as it is, but also how to understand the machinations of change. What has, or is, causing our society, our systems, and our policies to remain in status quo, and what is or has caused them to spring into reform?

Where and *When* give context and help provide meaning both to the learner and also to the learning community.

DOI: 10.4324/9781003228066-9

Place and Time

Learning must be meaningful to be worthwhile. Too often we relegate that meaning to the benchmark or the upcoming test. Rather than seek meaning or develop meaning of the learning in our students, we too often declare meaning (*you'll thank me later in life*) or worse still abdicate ourselves from any true meaning (*it's on the test*). Meaning itself must be understood and owned by the learner. That is not to say that the teacher cannot infuse or lead the learner to meaning, but ultimately for something to be meaningful it must be absorbed and have inherent worth. Its value must be understood by the learner and they must see its relevance to them, their lives, their world, or their future.

> . . . ultimately for something to be meaningful it must be absorbed and have inherent worth. Its value must be understood by the learner and they must see its relevance to them, their lives, their world, or their future.

It must relate to *their Where* and *their When*.

Place and time provide the most direct context for developing meaning. It aligns with learners' world, their neighborhood, their community, their interactions. It butts up against their current reality. Historical events track to their current understandings and their current world. They are not arbitrary incidents that occur in a far-off world but rather actions that led, either by happenstance or deliberately (or more likely somewhat in between the two), to where they and we are today. It provides a path and a map of relevance to the now, and as a consequence to the future.

The study of history is not the study of dates but rather the study of decisions and actions. When taught effectively, it places the learner in the role of an actor in a set of scenarios. What decision was made? What actions were made as a consequence? What influenced that decision? What contradicted that decision? What outcomes – unforeseen at the time – were unintended? What decision could have been made that may have had better outcomes? What actions could have been avoided or adjusted?

We learn about our history so that we both learn from successes and mistakes but also learn more about who we are collectively. *When* provides us with more detail about *Who* we are and *Why*.

These two sides of the history-coin were raised in discussion by Peter N. Stearns in his aptly named 'Why Study History?':

History Helps Us Understand People and Societies

Consequently, history must serve, however imperfectly, as our laboratory, and data from the past must serve as our most vital evidence in the unavoidable quest to figure out why our complex species behaves as it does in societal settings. This, fundamentally, is why we cannot stay away from history: it offers the only extensive evidential base for the contemplation and analysis of how societies function, and people need to have some sense of how societies function simply to run their own lives.

History Helps Us Understand Change and How the Society We Live in Came to Be

The past causes the present, and so the future. Any time we try to know why something happened—whether a shift in political party dominance in the American Congress, a major change in the teenage suicide rate, or a war in the Balkans or the Middle East—we have to look for factors that took shape earlier. Sometimes fairly recent history will suffice to explain a major development, but often we need to look further back to identify the causes of change.

Stearns (1998)[1]

Even a rudimentary review of History curricula in various countries will reveal that the local context is core and understanding how we came to be – as we are today – is what drives its rationale. We don't study Australian History typically in California as it doesn't have a direct relevance or need. Yet we do continue in elementary school to study the Greeks, Romans, and Egyptians, as they provide relevance to *Who* we are. History, our *When*, if crafted well becomes both a beacon illuminating our past but also a series of lessons from which we should learn as we plan our futures.

The problem however around our *When* and our context arises when sections of our community are left out of our history, or at least left out of the history content taught as *What* in many schools. Few schools and systems teach Indigenous history, even though in the US, Native Americans account for approximately 5.6 million or 2% of the population.[2] In Oklahoma, the Native American population rises to approximately 13% and in Alaska to approximately 20%. One could justify teaching Native American history as a way for our students to better understand *Who* they are but also to better understand *Who* we are.

What occurred to our Indigenous populations and why did this occur? What decisions were made and what actions occurred as a consequence? Would we make the same decisions now and if so, or if not, then why? Sweeping these discussions under the educational rug does nothing to help us know and learn about ourselves; it hides us from ourselves and prevents us from understanding others.

> Sweeping these discussions under the educational rug does nothing to help us know and learn about ourselves; it hides us from ourselves and prevents us from understanding others.

We have seen in recent months other topics of *When* that make up *Who* we are come into the public dialogue. The teaching of the Tulsa Race Massacre of 1921, when a white mob destroyed Tulsa's Greenwood District, also known as the Black Wall Street; and the 1691 Project, a *New York Times*, and *New York Times Magazine* joint project focusing on slavery from the slaves' perspective, have both been highly praised but also fervently criticized by portions of our society.

Too many of our own histories, and that of others, have been sanctioned away so as not to upset or distort our understanding of *Who* we are. But isn't that a core premise for why we learn history in the first place – to understand ourselves better? By ignoring or sanitizing

> By ignoring or sanitizing histories, we deprive our students, especially those who have been sanitized away from our texts, of relevance, and we deprive our collective selves of understanding *Who* we are better.

histories, we deprive our students, especially those who have been sanitized away from our texts, of relevance, and we deprive our collective selves of understanding *Who* we are better.

This is true of the Tulsa Race Massacre, which was rarely taught in schools prior to 2002. According to a recent survey of Oklahomans, 83% had never received a full lesson on the Tulsa Race Massacre or Black Wall Street during their K-12 school days, and 61% said they had only heard about them subsequently via news media.[3]

As Oklahoma state Senator Matthews, an African American politician who lives and was raised in the city, when learning about the incident in his thirties declared, "I call it a conspiracy of silence. It was purposely not talked about. It's almost like things that happen in your family that you're not proud of—people don't talk about it. I think it's something our city and state aren't that proud of and didn't want to talk about."[4]

Our *When* provides context to understanding *Who* we are and *Who* we want to become.

Culture and Context

Culture and context place the learning in a relevant frame. It aligns the learning to the learner's reality and by doing so makes connections into their world and their understandings. If we know that engagement in learning is directly related to its relevance and its meaning (to the learner), then ignoring the culture and context of the learning is paramount to ignoring effective pedagogy.

> Context changes and brings meaning—both shared and individual—to everything we see, hear, and experience. Yet, in education, both the idea and the teaching of context's power, is largely ignored. Rather than looking at the context, we focus on what lives inside the context itself: content and contest—the belief that by knowing a bunch of "stuff" and learning it in a competitive environment, a person will be able to successfully navigate the future. The educational system implicitly assumes that learning in one context easily transfers to other contexts and that it has established the best, most conducive context for learning.
>
> Pickering (2019)[5]

Where (place) and *When* (time) matter. And both place and time are brought together in the learning by the culture and context. Culture is both the location of a place as well as the people who make up that place. Together they intertwine. Context similarly brings in the current or recent events of that location and people. Culture and context make the learning relevant and meaningful to the learners. Too often, however, we as educators resort to our culture or our context as the prevailing culture and context.

> Too often, however, we as educators resort to our culture or our context as the prevailing culture and context.

Most of us in the education profession are white, middle-class, monolingual-English speakers. Increasingly, the same profile does not hold true for our students. Often, when we stand before our classrooms, the faces looking back at us do not look like our own. Many of us try to bridge this difference with an embrace of color-blindness or the Golden Rule, treating others the way we would want to be treated. But the truth is: culture matters.

Culture isn't just a list of holidays or shared recipes, religious traditions, or language; it is a lived experience unique to each individual. As educators, it's our job to stimulate the intellectual development of children, and, in this era, it's simply not enough to operate on the axis of color-blindness. To truly engage students, we must reach out to them in ways that are culturally and linguistically responsive and appropriate, and we must examine the cultural assumptions and stereotypes we bring into the classroom that may hinder interconnectedness.

Learning for Justice, formerly Teaching Tolerance[6]

Teaching Tolerance was a non-profit organization founded in 1991 by the Southern Poverty Law Center and has been recently renamed Learning for Justice to better reflect its mission. It has sought over the past 30 years to reduce prejudice and develop educational materials and programs to create inclusive school communities where children and youth across all cultures are respected, valued, and welcome participants in learning. The organization has made enormous headway in aligning learning with the culture and context of the learners.

For quite some time, Teaching Tolerance has subscribed to Emily Style's view that students need texts that are both "mirrors"—works in which they see themselves reflected—and "windows"—opportunities to look into the lives of others. Students who encounter a diverse mix of stories that are real and told from experience can learn to turn mirrors into windows and windows into mirrors…

…If we are to confront and heal the wounds that divide us as a society, we must be willing to listen to stories that are not like our own, and truly hear and believe them. We must do it for all students, regardless of color, income bracket, national origin, religion, language proficiency, ability, LGBT status or place on the gender spectrum. We must do it for our students whose parents' work in law enforcement and for our students whose parents might be behind bars. We must learn and teach them to ask each other, "What is it like to be you?"

Costello (2017)[7]

Teaching and learning in this way has a two-fold benefit. Firstly, it makes the learning relevant to those who are in the classroom, showing the context of their lives, their culture, and their reality. It directly aligns with learners' lives. But the second benefit is for those who have only read or seen examples of their own culture being introduced to another culture. It broadens their horizon and expands their understanding of the society we live in.

> It broadens their horizon and expands their understanding of the society we live in.

In Chapter 5, 'Who,' we introduced the work that Tom Hoerr did at The New School around multiple intelligences. Firstly, focus on the intelligence of strength to the learner. Draw them in, make the learning meaningful, allow them to thrive. But then they would focus on the weaker intelligences to allow those to grow and to allow the students to have to struggle. This focus on our own culture and then a focus on other cultures plays out the same process. Draw the learner in and make the learning relevant, logical, and aligned to the learner's experience. But then don't be afraid to push the learner out of their understanding or their comfort zone. The difference here is that the frame of reference is not multiple intelligences but multiple cultures.

Teaching Tolerance recently changed their name and the reason they did so is also worth repeating here as we explore culture and context as a theme. The name was changed as the times change and as our intended purpose changes. While 'tolerance' was seen as a valuable goal in the 1990s, it is seen as inadequate in the 2020s. Similarly, as 'teaching' was viewed previously as a core action, a better current objective is to focus on the 'learning' that the student is engaging. It can be viewed as word-smithing but words and terminology evoke meaning and the values we place on that learning. Why the change of name? The change of name fits exactly with our focus here on growing relevance and ownership in the learning. Teaching was taken out of the title because:

> [W]e want to recognize that we don't have all the answers. We want to name that we are learning alongside you as you work for the changes that students, families, educators and districts need to ensure that our schools are places where all students can thrive. Because we understand that this work will outlast us. And we want you to know that we promise to be in this work together with you. Because we want to honor this truth: that learning from—and with—one another is the first step to making justice real.
>
> Learning for Justice, formerly Teaching Tolerance[8]

Tolerance was replaced with justice as they are different entities. As was stated by Liles Dunn, the director of Learning for Justice, "The fact is, tolerance is not justice. It isn't a sufficient description of the work we do or of the world we want."

"The fact is, tolerance is not justice. It isn't a sufficient description of the work we do or of the world we want."

Tolerance can be defined as accepting or it can be defined as a "willingness to tolerate something, in particular the existence of opinions or behavior that one does not necessarily agree with" (Oxford Dictionary). Meaningful learning should be more than putting up with something, especially if that something is a culture. Striving for justice equates to the "quality of being fair and reasonable" (Oxford Dictionary).[9]

Relevance and Meaning

Why is relevance and meaning important? Because it relates to how our brains work and how we store, align, combine, and recall information.

There has been a boom in neurological study with regard to learning in recent years. What this is showing us is that when we are engaged in meaningful activities, we learn more. When we triangulate this learning with a variety of senses, we recall more.

> When we learn via a variety of styles and activities, we absorb more and as a result are able to align that new information better with previous information.

When we learn via a variety of styles and activities, we absorb more and as a result are able to align that new information better to previous information.

In short, neurological studies are showing that when students are engaged in relevant and meaningful activities, their learning is enhanced.

Stimulating the relevant cortex in the brain is key, but probably more important for both retention and relevance is the ability of the learner to relate this new learning to older information stored in the brain. The brain aligns or links new information with old information:

Neuroimaging and electroencephalography (EEG) brain mapping of subjects in the process of learning new information reveal that the most active areas of the brain when new sensory information is received are the somatosensory cortex areas. Input from each individual sense (hearing, touch, taste, vision, smell) is delivered to these areas and then matched with previously stored related memories. For example, the brain appears to link new words about cars with previously stored data in the category of transportation. Simultaneously, the limbic system, comprising parts of the temporal lobe, hippocampus, amygdala, and prefrontal cortex (front part of the frontal lobe), adds emotional significance to the information (sour flavor is tasty in lemon sherbet but unpleasant in spoiled juice).

Such relational memories appear to enhance storage of the new information in long-term memory.

Willis (2007)[10]

It also makes common sense. Effective teachers have been doing this for generations but without the science to back it up – rather, it was backed up by experience and real-time action research. We form understanding by aligning information with previous information. After time and effective contextual alignment, such understanding forms a picture. We grow and develop our understandings with new or additional information. Information that does not link or align to previous information is forgotten quicker or is more difficult to recall.

> Information that does not link or align with previous information is forgotten quicker or is more difficult to recall.

And as Judy Willis outlined above, aligning new information with varying senses (hearing, touch, taste, vision, smell) adds to the linking, alignment, and recall. More recent studies have found that emotions – positive and negative – also affect learning and recall. The study 'The Influences of Emotion on Learning and Memory' (Tyng, et al., 2017)[11] found that emotions can enhance and diminish learning and that the words used by the teacher during the lesson were frequently recalled along with the subject matter. "Emotion has a substantial influence on the cognitive processes in humans, including perception, attention, learning, memory, reasoning, and problem solving." And that emotion has "a particularly strong influence on attention, especially modulating the selectivity of attention as well as motivating action and behavior."[12] This is not to state categorically that positive emotions equate always with positive learning outcomes – as some studies show that stress and anxiety can also enhance learning – but it does highlight the relationship between emotions, meaningful engagement, and learning.

> . . . flow is encapsulated by engagement in an activity and as such must be owned and meaningful to the learner.

This study is also reminiscent of the work of the late Mihaly Csikszentmihalyi, who coined the term 'flow' for the ability to learn and be absorbed in an activity. Such flow is encapsulated by engagement in an activity and as such must be owned and meaningful to the learner.

Flow occurs when one is caught up in activity.

> It is when we act freely, for the sake of the action itself rather than for ulterior motives, that we learn to become more than what we were. When we choose a goal and invest ourselves in it to the limits of concentration, whatever we do will be enjoyable. And once we have tasted this joy, we will redouble our efforts to taste it again. This is the way the self grows.
>
> Csikszentmihalyi (1999)[13]

Flow is that state of forgetting time and being absorbed in an activity. In Csikszentmihalyi's words, flow is a "state in which people are so involved in an activity that nothing else seems to matter; the experience is so enjoyable that people will continue to do it even at great cost, for the sheer sake of doing it."[14]

Flow doesn't have to equate to pleasure in the fundamental sense of the word, nor does it relate to ease. Rather, it relates to being in the zone, often pushing yourself or at least being encapsulated in the activity. When flow occurs, it is also the setting for the most learning to occur. Why? Because you are engaged, and the activity has relevance to you. Your engagement is so great that you forget other distractions and as such you're focused on your actions and the consequences. It is a prime learning environment.

Now it is unlikely for us to replicate such situations in the classroom or in every learning environment, but we can learn from what and how we get into the flow. Csikszentmihalyi describes eight characteristics of flow, all of which can be absorbed into our teaching and more importantly our students' learning. These are reproduced below, together with my own reflections on how this relates to education.

1. Complete concentration on the task
   In order for one to focus and concentrate on a task it must have value and meaning, preferably intrinsic value or even extrinsic

(though this has been shown to be far less effective). Meaning and value relate back to relevance, which in turn relates back to culture and context.

2. Clarity of goals and reward in mind and immediate feedback
   Clarity of goals means that the learner understands the value and purpose of the activity as it relates to them. The activity also has a short-term outcome which is viewed as achievable.

3. Transformation of time (speeding up/slowing down)
   This is an indication of being in flow. Time is abstract.

4. The experience is intrinsically rewarding
   Meaning for the individual – they own the activity and seek its completion.

5. Effortlessness and ease
   While struggle can and often does precede flow, once the learner is in flow the path becomes smooth and things fall into place.

6. There is a balance between challenge and skills
   Flow is not always easy and often requires struggle or challenge. If something is too easy, it is not engaging. If it is too hard, it is difficult to maintain focus and achieve wins.

7. Actions and awareness are merged, losing self-conscious rumination
   One thinks and acts, responds, and adjusts.

8. There is a feeling of control over the task.
   There is not only ownership of the goal but ownership of the activity.

So, what are we seeking in our schools? Obedience to a set of systems, structures, and schedules marked out by benchmarks and graded along bell curves? Or are we seeking engagement in learning?

If we seek the latter, we should refocus our attention as educators on what fundamentals we need to establish in our schools to help that to occur. Take the last eight points. The fundamental basis for allowing flow to be part of our students' learning can only occur when the learning is

♦ Relevant
♦ Meaningful

- ◆ Contextualized
- ◆ Personalized
- ◆ Adjustable
- ◆ Malleable.

Where and When in the Classroom

Questions to ask yourself
- ◆ Am I able to adjust the content and skills currently being taught to make it more meaningful to my students?
- ◆ What content and skills would be most meaningful for my students?
- ◆ What content and skills are my students developing outside of school that I can enhance in my lessons?

Questions to ask your students
- ◆ How does this relate to your lives?
- ◆ Are there things that you can take from this that can have meaning?
- ◆ What do you know about this topic?
- ◆ What do your friends and family know?

Questions for your students to ask themselves
- ◆ Why was this included in the curriculum?
- ◆ What was its original or current purpose?
- ◆ How may this relate to your lives?
- ◆ If the purpose of the topic is (*fill in*) then what would be a more meaningful way to learn about it?

Notes

1   Stearns, P., 'Why Study History? (1998),' *American Historical Association*. www.historians.org/about-aha-and-membership/aha-history-and-archives/historical-archives/why-study-history-(1998)

2   US Census 2019 Data. https://data.census.gov/cedsci/table?q=American%20Indian%20and%20Alaska%20Native&tid=ACSDT1Y2019.B02010

3   Martinez-Keel, N., '"A Conspiracy of Silence": Tulsa Race Massacre Was Absent from Schools for Generations,' *The Oklahoman*, May 26, 2021. www.oklahoman.com/story/news/education/2021/05/26/ oklahoma-history-black-wall-street-left-out-public-schools-tulsa-massacre-education/4875340001/

4   Martinez-Keel, N., Ibid.

5   Pickering, T., 'How to Shift from Education as Content to Education as Context,' *Education Reimagined*, January 29, 2019. https:// education-reimagined.org/how-to-shift-from-education-as-content-to-education-as-context/

6   Learning for Justice, 'Culture in the Classroom.' www. learningforjustice.org/professional-development/culture-in-the-classroom

7   Costello, M., 'Perspectives,' *The Storytelling Issue, Teaching Tolerance* magazine, July 2017, p. 5. www.learningforjustice.org/sites/default/ files/2017-07/Teaching_Tolerance_Spring_2015.pdf

8   Learning for Justice, 'Our New Name: Learning for Justice,' February 3, 2021. www.learningforjustice.org/magazine/our-new-name-learning-for-justice

9   Oxford Dictionary, definitions of 'tolerance' and 'justice.' www. oxfordlearnersdictionaries.com/us/definition/english/tolerance; www.oxfordlearnersdictionaries.com/us/definition/english/justice

10   Willis, J., 'The Neuroscience of Joyful Education,' *Educational Leadership*, Vol. 64 (Summer 2007), Engaging the Whole Child. www.psychologytoday.com/files/attachments/4141/the-neuroscience-joyful-education-judy-willis-md.pdf

11   Tyng, C., Amin, H., Saad, M., & Malik, A., 'The Influences of Emotion on Learning and Memory,' *Frontiers in Psychology*, Vol. 8 (2017): 1454. https://doi.org./10.3389/fpsyg.2017.01454

12   Tyng, C., et al., Ibid.

13   Csikszentmihalyi, M., *Flow: The Psychology of Optimal Experience*, Harper and Row, 1999, pp. 42–43.

14   Csikszentmihalyi, M., Ibid., p. 4.

7

How and What

What content we learn, and what skills we learn, must be aligned to the previous questions of *Why, Who, When,* and *Where*. Without this pathway the learning becomes disjointed from purpose and disconnected from the learner. It quickly becomes a task or series of tasks, as opposed to learning and self-improvement.

Relevance used to be – and in many places still is – joined to social progression. The value of what was being learned was less important or relevant than the fact that moving though this system successfully equated to an increase in social status and livelihood. Graduation, a college degree, all resulted in a higher standing socially.

Relevance then was equated more directly with economic gain, with the message being that a graduate would earn more than a non-graduate. Subsequently, a diploma and degree would equate to higher incomes. All this is true and is still true today. However, as our world changes and our economic needs evolve, the myth that an education will automatically lead to a full-time job and a successful career is becoming less and less true.

> . . . as our world changes and our economic needs evolve, the myth that an education will automatically lead to a full-time job and a successful career is becoming less and less true.

Graduation, diplomas, and degrees significantly improve your chances, but it no longer guarantees a livelihood.

Why? Because the content and skills taught are becoming less relevant to the modern world and less meaningful to the learner.

DOI: 10.4324/9781003228066-10

> Because the gap between what is needed and what is taught (or learned) is becoming wider.

Because the gap between what is needed and what is taught (or learned) is becoming wider. Because we still teach much of the same content and skills that we taught decades ago.

This growing dilemma, however, has presented us with an opportune moment to reassess what we are teaching and why.

3 R's

The basis for learning – the ability to read, write, and conduct arithmetic – are not in dispute. They are the foundation that every learner must learn. However, the early insistence we place upon them, the way we have taught them, and the way we have structured their learning, can and must be improved.

For too many students these *What*'s and *How*'s are too often disjointed from other learning. They have been set up as basics – building blocks as the analogy – to be learned and mastered, one step at a time, before other learning takes place. It is a constructionist (not constructivist) process of learning. Learn the basics, then use them, step by step for other activities and experiences.

The bricks come first, and the buildings come second. If you get distracted, bored, or disengaged by the process, then sorry you must go back and try again. You don't get to pass 'Go' and you don't get to 'collect your $200' (this is a *Monopoly* reference for those who may not be familiar).

> The bricks come first, and the buildings come second. If you get distracted, bored, or disengaged by the process, then sorry you must go back and try again.

While this initial learning process can work for many students, it doesn't for every student and especially those for whom English is a second language or who come from homes where reading isn't practiced frequently. In such homes where reading is commonplace, the content and skills of reading, writing, and arithmetic are able to be practiced more often and placed into a real-world context. As such it becomes more meaningful and more purposeful. For those who struggle with mastering the building blocks and don't have opportunities to practice or apply this learning in their real world, it remains merely a set of bricks. The learning becomes absent from meaning and absent from their reality.

Cast your mind back to when you were in school and perhaps being asked to memorize a math formula or a physics calculation. While I was good at Math in primary/elementary school, I soon lost interest in high school because the meaning or purpose of it was disengaged from the process. Whereas my teachers, and the level of the math in primary/elementary school, meant that I could understand the relevance, it became ever murkier in high school to the point where I was struggling. I was doing mathematical equations for the sake of doing mathematical equations. I lost my relevance and engagement with the *What*'s and *How*'s.

Better teachers, or perhaps a more enlightened student, may have been able to see the value in thinking abstractly, in solving problems based on a specific formula, in seeing the connections between seeking solutions and the world around us. But that wasn't me, nor my teachers at the time. It was 'do it for the sake of doing it.' Compliance was expected; curiosity wasn't.

> It was 'do it for the sake of doing it.' Compliance was expected; curiosity wasn't.

That is the same as many of our students feel as they are asked to learn the building blocks of reading, writing, and numeracy, before they have deliberate opportunities to learn it through and via discovery of other topics and skills. While young learners are resilient, they can also lose interest, or perhaps rather lose the opportunity to spark their curiosity. As such students who grow disengaged soon grow disillusioned with education writ large.

A couple of years ago I had the opportunity to meet Yong Zhao, author of many books but at the time he had just published *Catching Up or Leading the Way: American Education in the Age of Globalization*, where he compared and contrasted the varying methods and views in education from West to East. I raise it here because he recalls a wonderful chat he had with his then child's first grade teacher.

"Children are like popcorn," Mrs. Lippe, my son's 1st grade teacher, told me at a parent-teacher conference. "They all pop, some sooner and some later," she added, "but in the end, they all pop." Mrs. Lippe's words are still fresh in my mind after almost 10 years. During those 10 years, I have met many teachers in different situations, including those who took my classes, attended my lectures, joined international study tours I led, and, of course, taught my two children. I found that Mrs. Lippe's view of children is shared by many of the teachers I have interacted with in the United States.

Zhao (2009)[1]

All children pop. All children will get the concepts and learnings – some sooner, some later – but they will all get it. I think that view is held by many teachers and

> All children pop. All children will get the concepts and learnings – some sooner, some later – but they will all get it.

most educators; however, our systems often work against this approach, demanding the child hit a set of focused benchmarks by a certain grade. Out with the popcorn approach and back to constructing knowledge brick by brick. Every student will pop at a certain time given the appropriate environment and learning opportunities. What we should be doing is developing these learning environments and at the same time not allowing the child's curiosity to be dampened.

If we keep education meaningful and relevant, the learner learns. If we keep curiosity as a driver, the learner wants to learn. If we keep the discovery of things, as well as who we are, as a core function of education, the learner discovers. Unfortunately, we often do more of the opposite and then expect the learner to be engaged, motivated, and committed.

Engagement isn't a compliable action that the learner can switch on or off. Paying attention is or listening is, as these are mere

> Engagement isn't a compliable action that the learner can switch on or off.

actions, but engagement requires the learning itself to be worth engaging with and meaningful. Engagement is the outcome of an engaging activity. One cannot just say you must or will be engaged; the teacher as the pedagogical expert must craft the learning to encapsulate interest and illustrate relevance.

Here is one other example from Yong Zhao's book that exemplifies this.

It was an exciting day for the children at Central Elementary School in Okemos, Michigan. They had two opportunities to show their talents to their parents, friends, siblings, and classmates—one in the afternoon and one in the evening. I was invited to attend the evening performance by my 5th grade daughter. For about an hour, my wife and I, together with about 100 other parents, watched, laughed, and applauded as the show went on in the school gym with a makeshift stage. The 3rd, 4th, and 5th graders displayed their talents: singing, dancing, karate, piano, violin, drum, fashion show—anything as long as it was "G-rated," according to my 9-year-old. The event was funny, amusing, mesmerizing, and pride-invoking for the adults, but dead serious for the children. The performances were of uneven quality, as one might expect. Some were pretty good, but most were not that great. Nonetheless, all the performers won enthusiastic applause from the audience. This was not the first time I had attended such an event involving my children. This was, I am certain, not the only such school event happening all around the country on that day. But every time I attend an event like this, I cannot help but discuss with my wife the differences between education in China and the United States. Both my wife and I were born in China and went through the Chinese education system, although in different situations. I attended a very impoverished rural village school, whereas she attended a much better school in a large city. All the students in my school were children of peasants, and most of the students in her school were children of college professors. But surprisingly, our reflections on the talent show were almost identical. What struck us most is the lack of standards in these talent shows. There was no selection process to decide who was qualified to enter the show. All students in the three grades were invited and could enter the show if they filled out a form. The short audition was simply to let the organizers know what each student was planning to do. There was no judge, no assessment of the performance during the show. No prize or award was given after the show, either. But all the performers took the show seriously, dressed in their best, and some even appeared nervous. No doubt they worked very hard to win over the audience and took great pride in their "talents." And they were all rewarded. Regardless of what and how they performed, they received loud applause for their effort.

Zhao (2009)[2]

What do we want students to learn? – perseverance, persistence, practice, self-expression, confronting self-doubt, changing self-efficacy, communication, expression, the list could go on. All of these skills were being taught in the instance described in Yong Zhao's book and were likely also sparking interest and curiosity in both the performers and the audience.

Meaning Related to the Learner

Common themes keep coming up both in this book and in the world of pedagogy. Purpose, meaning, engagement, relevance, ownership, agency, and personalization are all areas cited for improving learning. One often is required for the other, or at a minimum, leads onto the other.

And if we listed these areas, they would align with the core tenets of our new solar system, especially *Why* and *Who*, and spanning into the *Where and When*, and *How and What*.

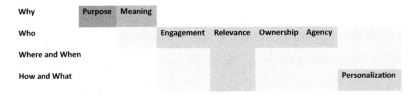

Why	**Purpose**	**Meaning**				
Who			Engagement	Relevance	Ownership	Agency
Where and When						
How and What						Personalization

Or if we placed these areas into and across our solar system, they would span and interact across a number of orbits from *Why* through to *What*.

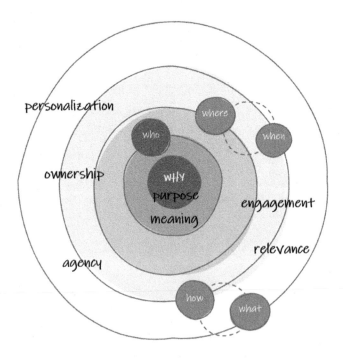

What has become clearer as we have travelled through our old educational solar systems is that if you ignore the rationale for learning and bypass the initial steps for making it purposeful and meaningful, it's very difficult to address the next set of criteria – from engagement, relevance, ownership, agency, through to personalization.

> . . . that if you ignore the rationale for learning and bypass the initial steps for making it purposeful and meaningful, it's very difficult to address the next set of criteria . . .

If the core of your solar system is the *What* followed by the *How*, your personalization becomes personalization of a learning style at best. We struggle to effectively personalize because we have foregone the initial foray into our *Why* and *Who*. Personalization, along with the areas of engagement, relevance, ownership, and agency, become watered-down versions at best and struggle to address the needs and interests of the learner. The agency-creating elements of 'choice and voice' become a list of predetermined topics to study. Ownership becomes a time-stamped project or an extra-curricular activity.

Content and Skills with a Purpose

> There is a time and a place for content and skills – but we first need to ask ourselves and understand *Why* they are needed.

There is a time and a place for content and skills – but we first need to ask ourselves and understand *Why* they are needed. This does not mean that every piece of content nor every skill must have a discrete goal. Content (*What*) can be learned to aid the development of skills. Skills (*How*) can be learned to further a mastery of content. But neither should be absent from our original *Why* and *Who*.

In addition to learning content for skills development, content can also be learned to foster an understanding of *Who* we are or *Who* we may become. Extending our understanding of ourselves and what we are capable of is a core function of education – but ultimately it is tied to a purpose.

The purpose (*Why*) can be understanding the rationale in something. It can be *Who*, developing a greater understanding of who we are individually and collectively. It can also serve – as it does primarily now – to enhance our own ability to grow and develop our careers. There is a valid purpose and process to learn new content, new concepts, and new skills.

Many of us have developed a better appreciation of who we are and what we are capable of via the current school system. It pushes us with regard to self-efficacy and perseverance. It allows us to experience a range of activities and trains us in a series of set skills. All of this is fine – the issue is that all of this is set somewhat arbitrarily, and divorced from what we know works in effective pedagogy. At best most students discover something they enjoy or find interesting that they may wish to continue with into adulthood or university. They discover something acceptable. A few students become engrossed and engaged in the lessons; but the majority seek without finding a passion, or even a purpose, in what they are being asked to learn.

My rationale here is not that *What* and *How* should be ignored or discarded – in fact, far from it. My rationale here is that *What* and *How* must align back to the previous questions starting with *Why* and *Who*, and then contextualized by *Where* and *When*. Establish the purpose, develop the ownership, grow the agency, craft the learning.

> *What* and *How* must align back to the previous questions starting with *Why* and *Who*, and then contextualized by *Where* and *When*. Establish the purpose, develop the ownership, grow the agency, and craft the learning.

Skills Needed and in Demand

There are also however a range of skills that are both in demand by industry, and also skills that help us determine and develop *Who* we are. These skills are not tied to outdated industries and should be in demand for years to come.

These skills that have for years been called 'soft skills' and are the skills needed to adjust and adapt to changing environments. These skills allow us to work better together and to solve problems.

> Soft skills… encompass creativity, problem solving and creating meaning, and use the processes of communication, personal and group interaction, and consensus building. They encapsulate an understanding of group dynamics, of social and emotional wellbeing, and of team building.
>
> Yet they are not the 'nice to have' skills, but rather the 'must have' skills. The way we use information in the future, creating new meanings and new ideas, will be critical. Information is important but, in this century, the role of utilising that information and adapting it to new and varied situations will be paramount.
>
> Slade & Lambert (2019)[3]

In our paper, *Reclaiming, Reprioritising, Reassessing and Recasting 'Soft Skills'*, we called for the reclaiming of these skills and the term 'soft skills' by the education community as they encompass

> Soft skills are fluid, malleable, adjustable, and adaptable. They can be used across a multitude of situations and circumstances, time and time again.

> **Soft skills** – fluid, malleable, adjustable, suited to multiple situations and circumstances. They adapt, change, and grow. They morph, are usable and fit (because they are fluid) into every arena. They are a necessity for everyone. Think fluid, think liquid, think water.

> **Hard skills** – static, non-dynamic, heavy, old. These skills constrict usage, trap the development of new meanings inside a subject area, and create barriers to new knowledge or alternative ways of thinking. Think old school building, bricks, mortar, memorising times tables.

Slade & Lambert [i]

Slade, S. & Lambert, P., *Reclaiming, Reprioritising, Reassessing and Recasting 'Soft Skills,'* Centre for Strategic Education Seminar Series Paper #288, September 2019.

what is needed as we enter a more VUCA – volatile, uncertain, complex, ambiguous – world. Soft skills are fluid, malleable, adjustable, and adaptable. They can be used across a multitude of situations and circumstances, time and time again.

They fill the spaces left by the rigid frame of standard hard skills, making sense of the information and in turn flowing into new and unexpected meaning. Hard skills, those defined by facts and testable information, instead can be illustrated as old, heavy, non-dynamic, static, and not suited (nor needed) for every situation.

We are not alone in this push. Such skills have been raised and advocated for by many of the world's leading economic and educational entities, from the research thinktank, The Brookings Institution, to the education forecasting organization, KnowledgeWorks, to global entities such as UNESCO, these skills have been highlighted as skills needed for the future.

The Brookings Institution[4]

◆ Critical and innovative thinking
◆ Interpersonal skills
◆ Intrapersonal skills
◆ Global citizenship
◆ Physical and psychological health

KnowledgeWorks[5]

◆ Deep self-knowledge
◆ Emotional regulation
◆ Empathy and perspective taking

UNESCO[6]

♦ Collaboration
♦ Communication
♦ Social and/or cultural competencies (including citizenship)

In fact, for anyone who has been involved in education forecasting, or indeed for anyone engaged in the business community, the clarion call for a focus on the competencies of critical thinking, communication, collaboration, and creativity has been loud and clear. These 'soft skills' (utilizing our call to reclaim this term), or what the Partnership for 21st Century Learning called the 4 C's, has been on the rise since the end of the last century. As early as 1981, with the creation of the National Commission on Excellence in Education tasked to examine the quality of education in the United States, there was interest in determining the skills and competencies needed for the new upcoming century. The commission's report, *A Nation at Risk: The Imperative for Educational Reform* (1983),[7] outlined areas of new need, to complement traditional content and skills (read literacy and numeracy). While wrapped in a cloak of apprehension and concern about other countries overtaking the US in economic terms, and a consistent call for greater effort, the report also called for the development of a learning society.

> In a world of ever-accelerating competition and change in the conditions of the workplace, of ever-greater danger, and of ever-larger opportunities for those prepared to meet them, educational reform should focus on the goal of creating a Learning Society. At the heart of such a society is the commitment to a set of values and to a system of education that affords all members the opportunity to stretch their minds to full capacity, from early childhood through adulthood, learning more as the world itself changes. Such a society has as a basic foundation the idea that education is important not only because of what it contributes to one's career goals but also because of the value it adds to the general quality of one's life. Also at the heart of the Learning Society are educational opportunities extending

far beyond the traditional institutions of learning, our schools and colleges. They extend into homes and workplaces; into libraries, art galleries, museums, and science centers; indeed, into every place where the individual can develop and mature in work and life. In our view, formal schooling in youth is the essential foundation for learning throughout one's life. But without life-long learning, one's skills will become rapidly dated.

National Commission on Excellence in Education (1983)[8]

The economic and business community has also for many years been touting the desire, and in fact need, to focus more on these human interaction skills. The World Economic Forum has been listing desired skills for the future, outlining and forecasting where industry and the economy are heading and what skills

	2015	2020	2025
1	Complex problem solving (S, Soft)	Complex problem solving (S, Soft)	Analytical thinking and innovation (S, Soft)
2	Coordinating with others (O, Soft)	Critical thinking (S, Soft)	Active learning and learning strategies (S, Soft)
3	People management (O, Soft)	Creativity (S, Soft)	Complex problem solving (S, Soft)
4	Critical thinking (S, Soft)	People management (O, Soft)	Critical thinking and analysis (S, Soft)
5	Negotiation (O, Soft)	Coordinating with others (O, Soft)	Creativity, originality, and initiative (S, Soft)
6	Quality control (T, Hard)	Emotional intelligence (S, Soft)	Leadership and social influence (O, Soft)
7	Service orientation (O, Soft)	Judgement and decision making (S, Soft)	Technology use, monitoring, and control (T, Hard)
8	Judgement and decision making (S, Soft)	Service orientation (O, Soft)	Technology design and programming (T, Hard)
9	Active listening (S, Soft)	Negotiation (O, Soft)	Resilience, stress tolerance, and flexibility (S, Soft)
10	Creativity (S, Soft)	Cognitive flexibility (S, Soft)	Reasoning, problem solving, and ideation (S, Soft)

Top ten skills needed in 2015, 2020, and 2025

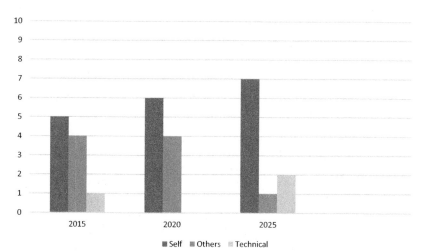

Top ten skills needed by 2015, 2020, and 2025 by categorization type

schools and universities should be focusing on. The following table is compiled from the World Economic Forum series, the *Future of Jobs Report* (2018[9]; 2020[10]); the information highlights this need for a greater focus on 'soft skills.'

If we categorize these skills by Self (S) skills, Skills for interacting with Others (O), or Technical skills (T), as I have done in the table, we see that the majority of skills are

- ◆ Self – 2015 (5); 2020 (6); 2025 (7)
- ◆ Others – 2015 (4); 2020 (4); 2025 (1)
- ◆ Technical – 2015 (1); 2020 (0); 2025 (2).

If we further list those by hard or soft skills, the evidence strongly suggests we are already in an era where soft is king – in fact, the battle has been over for a while and it wasn't even close. All that remains is for our education systems to catch up.

And what skills are in decline, meaning less need, and use for? This was the list from the recent World Economic Forum *Future of Jobs Report 2018*.[11] The categorization of Self (S), Others (O), and Technical (T) are my own, as is the listing of Hard versus Soft.

- ◆ Manual dexterity, endurance, and precision (T, Hard)
- ◆ Memory, verbal, auditory, and spatial abilities (S, Hard)

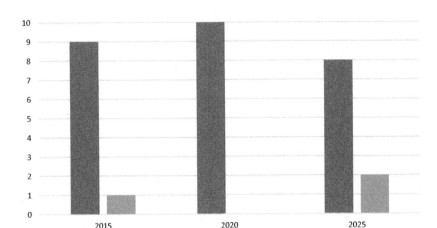

Top ten skills needed by 2015, 2020, and 2025 by Hard versus Soft

- ◆ Management of financial, material resources (T, Hard)
- ◆ Technology installation, and maintenance (T, Hard)
- ◆ Reading, writing, math, and active listening (T, Hard)
- ◆ Management of personnel (O, Hard/Soft)
- ◆ Quality control and safety awareness (T, Hard)
- ◆ Coordination and time management (S, Hard/Soft)
- ◆ Visual, auditory, and speech abilities (S, Hard/Soft)
- ◆ Technology use, monitoring, and control (T, Hard)

> We are seeing a declining need for hard skills and an increasing demand for soft skills.

We are seeing a declining need for hard skills and an increasing demand for soft skills. Even those that I have categorized as Hard/Soft are not distinctly soft skills only and have core technical elements. The underlying premise here is that soft skills – skills that are person oriented, malleable, suitable across industries, skills that focus on collaboration, cooperation, enterprise, communication, problem solving, and resilience – are in demand and will continue to grow in need. Hard skills – especially technical skills for certain industries – won't be forgotten or discarded, but they will be required less as the need for soft skills grows.

Summarized and placed together from two of the leading economic and education organizations globally, these statements echo the same call.

> Students will need to apply their knowledge in unknown and evolving circumstances. For this, they will need a broad range of skills, including cognitive and meta-cognitive skills (e.g., critical thinking, creative thinking, learning to learn and self-regulation); social and emotional skills (e.g., empathy, self-efficacy and collaboration); and practical and physical skills (e.g., using new information and communication technology devices).
>
> OECD (2018)[12]

Our education systems need to change and need to refocus their attention upon what has been deemed 'soft' in previous narratives because as UNESCO note, "Without a definitive paradigm shift, many curricula will continue to fail to facilitate learning, they will continue to register poor learning outcomes, and they will remain irrelevant for the future" (UNESCO, 2017).[13]

What and How in the Classroom

Questions to ask yourself

♦ How does what I am teaching reflect the skills and content needed in society and in the future?

♦ Am I aiding or hindering my students?

♦ What changes in approach and pedagogy can I make that would improve or enhance the skills being learned?

♦ How can I best draw out and emphasize the 'soft skills' needed while also adhering to the current benchmark requirements?

Questions to ask your students

♦ How does what we are learning in this subject area relate to other subject areas?

♦ Are there similarities or connections in content, or in how it is being taught/learnt (pedagogy)?

♦ Are there similarities across subject areas in the skills being learnt?

♦ How will this help you in the future? Turn the discussion towards the students to determine how/if what is being taught will have relevance. The answer is that every 'soft skill' can be taught via any content area, so the skills of problem solving, collaboration, and creativity may come out via the process rather than via the content being learned.

Questions for your students to ask themselves

♦ What skills and content do you think will have the greatest need in the future?

♦ How does what we are learning relate back to you and your context?

♦ What do you want to learn (content/skills) that has relevance to you and your context?

♦ How can you enhance or further develop your 'soft skills' outside of school?

◆ Are there times when you are practicing these skills that are harder/easier (e.g., home, friends, sports)? What makes it harder/easier and what can you learn from those experiences?

Notes

1   Zhao, Y., *Catching Up or Leading the Way: American Education in the Age of Globalization*, ASCD, 2009, p. 56.

2   Zhao, Y., Ibid., pp. 49–51.

3   Slade, S. & Lambert, P., *Reclaiming, Reprioritising, Reassessing and Recasting 'Soft Skills'*, Centre for Strategic Education Seminar Series Paper #288, September 2019, p.10.

4   Care, E., Kim, H, Vista, A., & Anderson, K., 'Education System Alignment for 21st Century Skills – Focus on Assessment,' The Brookings Institution, January 30, 2019. www.brookings.edu/research/education-system-alignment-for-21st-century-skills

5   Prince, K. & Swanson, J.,'The Future of Learning: Redefining Readiness from the Inside Out,' *KnowledgeWorks*, 2017. https://knowledgeworks.org/resources/future-learning-redefining-readiness/

6   UNESCO & International Bureau of Education, 'Twenty-first Century Skills.' www.ibe.unesco.org/en/glossary-curriculum-terminology/t/twenty-first-century-skills

7   National Commission on Excellence in Education, *A Nation at Risk: The Imperative for Educational Reform. A Report to the Nation and the Secretary of Education United States Department of Education by The National Commission on Excellence in Education*, The National Commission on Excellence in Education, April 1983, p. 14. https://edreform.com/wp-content/uploads/2013/02/A_Nation_At_Risk_1983.pdf

8   Partnership for 21st Century Learning (P21). https://education-reimagined.org/resources/partnership-for-21st-century-learning/

9   World Economic Forum, *The Future of Jobs Report 2018*. www3.weforum.org/docs/WEF_Future_of_Jobs_2018.pdf

10 World Economic Forum, *The Future of Jobs Report 2020*. www3.weforum.org/docs/WEF_Future_of_Jobs_2020.pdf

11   *The Future of Jobs Report 2018*, Ibid.

12   Organization for Economic Cooperation and Development (OECD), *The Future of Education and Skills: Education 2030*, 2018. www.oecd. org/education/2030-project/contact/E2030%20Position%20 Paper%20(05.04.2018).pdf

13   Marope, M., *Reconceptualizing and Repositioning Curriculum in the 21st Century: A Global Paradigm Shift*, 2017. www.ibe.unesco. org/sites/default/files/resources/reconceptualizing_and_ repositioning.pdf

Part 3

A Flipped Solar System

I am not anti-content, nor anti-skills, and not even anti-benchmarks, but I am opposed to how we have constructed our education system(s) without truly tackling the funda-

> We should all be protagonists of curiosity, and all educators should be curiosity drivers.

mental question of *Why*. What I am, however, is anti anti-purpose or anti anti-curiosity. Or to put it in a better, and more grammatically correct, way, I am 'pro-purpose' and 'pro-curiosity.' We should all be protagonists of curiosity, and all educators should be curiosity drivers.

We have abdicated ourselves from the discussion of 'why do we have an education system' or alternatively we have just supposed that the discussion is being had somewhere higher up in board rooms and meeting rooms where the likes of us should never dare to enter. The truth is that at these meetings such discussions are rarely had and if they are, they are typically only in the faculty rooms at progressive universities or think tanks.

What is discussed in the board rooms and meeting rooms – and typically by politicians and departmental staff – are accountability measures, benchmarking targets, graduation requirements, class-size requirements, seat-time requirements, all of which are aligned with the current system and current outcomes based on a selection of current *What*'s and *How*'s. The discussion debating the purpose of education and its misalignment with our current system is too often left well alone.

DOI: 10.4324/9781003228066-11

MS – The Wizard at the controls – his back to camera – he speaks into the microphone – he turns, looks o.s. to f.g. and sees that the curtain is gone – reacts and turns back to the controls –

OZ'S VOICE
…twenty years from now. Oh – oh oh!
The Great Oz has spoken! Oh – Oh –….

LS – Shooting past the Four at left to the Wizard as he pulls back the curtain –

OZ'S VOICE
… Oh …. Oh ….

MS – The Wizard peers out from behind the curtain –

MS – Tin Man, Lion, Dorothy and Scarecrow react as they look at the Wizard
o.s. to right – Dorothy speaks

DOROTHY
Who are you?

MCU – The Wizard peering out from curtain – he ducks back out of sight and his voice booms out again –

OZ'S VOICE
Oh – I – Pay no….

LS – Shooting past the Four at left to the Curtain in b.g. – Dorothy goes over to it and starts to pull it aside –

OZ'S VOICE
…attention to that man behind the curtain.

Go – before I lose my temper! The Great and Powerful –….

MCS – Dorothy pulls back the curtain to reveal the Wizard at the controls
– he reacts as he sees Dorothy – Dorothy questions him – the Wizard starts to speak into the microphone – then turns weakly back to Dorothy –

CAMERA PULLS back slightly as the Lion, Scarecrow and Tin Man enter and stand behind Dorothy –

OZ'S VOICE

… – Oz – has spoken!

DOROTHY

Who are you?

OZ'S VOICE

Well, I – I – I am the Great and Powerful – Wizard of Oz.

DOROTHY

You are?

WIZARD

Uhhhh – yes…

DOROTHY

I don't believe you!

WIZARD

No, I'm afraid it's true. There's no other Wizard except me.

The Wizard of Oz (1939)[1]

So, if we have not been having this discussion, how do we start? We start by flipping the educational solar system and place *Why* and *Who* before anything else. By placing these formative questions at the start, we reframe our actions and expectations. We reframe our rationale for why we are educating, and we change our mindsets. As such even if we don't immediately change our structures, we affect what we do in the classroom and why we do it.

By raising both *Why* and *Who* to the fore we start to affect our systems, our teaching and learning, and our students themselves. We start to ask continuous questions about what we are doing and why we are doing it. In turn, we enable and develop the passion of inquiry and curiosity in our students. People often react by

> By raising both *Why* and *Who* to the fore we start to affect our systems, our teaching and learning, and our students themselves.

seeing this type of questioning as an extra or additional task that they have little time for. However, by asking such questions of yourself and your peers, you begin to coalesce around a common focus. Teaching without a clear focus or a clear rationale means that you are constantly seeking to justify the reason and purpose or more likely just hope the questions of 'why do we need to know this?' never arise.

Think of this journey through the new educational solar system as a map with a path. Rather than being flung into space without guidance or more typically staring only at the sun of *What* (content), you are being guided from planet to planet in accordance with relevance.

Staying in our current status and orbit – revolving around the central star or the sun of *What* – will soon be terminal. This sun of *What* is increasing in size daily, hourly, and soon it will have an even greater influence and a greater gravitational pull on us. This

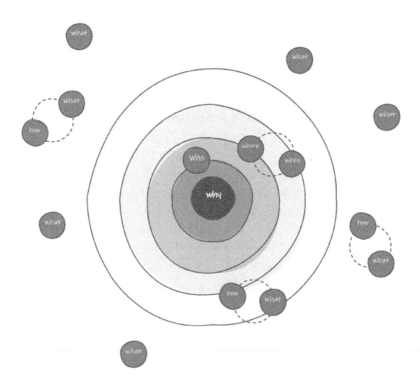

sun of *What* – as it grows larger – diminishes the pull of the other planets and quickly becomes the dominant or only real force in the solar system.

Taking our new solar system analogy, the central star or sun, *Why*, is constant but also ever changing. Its pull is there and central, but its influence consistent. *Why* – our reason for learning something – will morph and change, evolve, diminish, and grow – but its presence will remain constant and necessary.

What and *How* – now placed at the outer regions of the solar system – remain and also increase as the amount of information, data, and content increases. But rather than increase in size, perhaps it is better to think of them as a series of planets extending further out into space to be visited and encountered when needed. Their number increases but their pull remains isolated.

In order for us to understand and maintain this new solar system, there are questions we should be asking ourselves consistently, and they relate to our systems, our practice, and ultimately our learners,

> In order for us to understand and maintain this new solar system, there are questions we should be asking ourselves consistently. . .

who are moved via this questioning from a passive receiver of information to a cocreator of learning and a protagonist in inquiry and a steward of curiosity.

Systems
♦ Why do we have an education system and what do we want our children to gain from it?
♦ Why do we have an education system and what do we want our society to gain from it?
♦ Who are we becoming?

Teaching and learning
♦ Why am I teaching this?
♦ What do I want my students to gain from it?
♦ Who are they becoming?

Learner

- ◆ Why is this so?
- ◆ Why does/doesn't this make sense/work?
- ◆ Who am I becoming?

Note

1   *Wizard of Oz*, 1939. https://sfy.ru/script/wizard_of_oz_1939

Questions

This is a compilation of the questions asked of ourselves, our students, and by the students themselves throughout this *Questioning Education* book. These aren't the only questions to ask and as you can see by reading through them, they overlap and align regularly. The premise of all these questions is to go back to the start and ask ourselves why we are teaching and what we want our students to get out of the experience.

But it is not only up to us. Students themselves want to learn and want to know why or how it will be beneficial. Don't be afraid to say, 'I don't know' but follow it up with a 'What do you think?' and engage them in their own discovery. Aim to be the Little Prince rather than the serious man.

> Aim to be the Little Prince rather than the serious man.

"Hmm? You're still there? Five-hundred-and-one million… I don't remember … I have so much work to do! I'm a serious man. I can't be bothered with trifles! Two and five, seven…"

"Five-hundred-and-one million what?" Repeated the little prince, who had never in his life let go of a question once he has asked it.

The Little Prince (1943)[1]

And aim to be Dorothy rather than the Wizard.

DOI: 10.4324/9781003228066-12

> And aim to be Dorothy rather than the Wizard.

DOROTHY

Oh, dear – that's too wonderful to be true! Oh, it's – it's going to be so hard to say goodbye. I love you all, too. Goodbye, Tin Man. Oh, don't cry. You'll rust so dreadfully. Here – here's your oil-can. Goodbye.

TIN MAN

Now I know I've got a heart – 'cause it's breaking.

DOROTHY

Oh – Goodbye, Lion. You know, I know it isn't right, but I'm going to miss the way you used to holler for help before you found your courage.

LION

Well – I would never've found it if it hadn't been for you.[2]

Why in the Classroom

Questions to ask yourself
- ◆ Why did I become an educator?
- ◆ Why did I get into the profession in the first place?
- ◆ Do I still believe this to be true? If not, why not?
- ◆ What do I want my students to gain from my efforts?

Questions to ask your students
- ◆ What have you learned to do this [topic/unit/activity] that surprised you?
- ◆ What would you like to learn from our time together this year? Don't restrict your answers to only content (*What*) or skills (*How*).

Questions for your students to ask themselves
- ◆ We require children to go to school for 9–12 years. Why do we do this? What do we want them to develop?
- ◆ What in our current school system helps this?
- ◆ If you were inventing a school from scratch, what would you start with and focus on?

Who in the Classroom

Questions to ask yourself

- ◆ How have my experiences in and out of school changed or affected who I am?
- ◆ What experiences do I want to craft to allow my students to learn who they are?
- ◆ Does how I teach authentically reflect who I am?

Questions to ask your students

- ◆ What did you discover about yourself during that last [topic/unit/activity]?
- ◆ Was there anything that surprised you?
- ◆ How has your understanding of yourself changed over the last year?
- ◆ Is there anything about what you discovered that you can use in other parts of your life?

Questions for your students to ask themselves

- ◆ This is as much about determining who we are {plural} as it is about discovering who we each are {singular}. Who do you want us to be or become?
- ◆ What role can you play in helping us get there?

Where and When in the Classroom

Questions to ask yourself
♦ Am I able to adjust the content and skills currently being taught to make it more meaningful to my students?
♦ What content and skills would be most meaningful for my students?
♦ What content and skills are my students developing outside of school that I can enhance in my lessons?

Questions to ask your students
♦ How does this relate to your lives?
♦ Are there things that you can take from this that can have meaning?
♦ What do you know about this topic?
♦ What do your friends and family know?

Questions for your students to ask themselves
♦ Why was this included in the curriculum?
♦ What was its original or current purpose?
♦ How may this relate to your lives?
♦ If the purpose of the topic is (*fill in*) then what would be a more meaningful way to learn about it?

What and How in the Classroom

Questions to ask yourself

- ◆ How does what I am teaching reflect the skills and content needed in society and in the future?
- ◆ Am I aiding or hindering my students?
- ◆ What changes in approach and pedagogy can I make that would improve or enhance the skills being learned?
- ◆ How can I best draw out and emphasize the 'soft skills' needed while also adhering to the current benchmark requirements?

Questions to ask your students

- ◆ How does what we are learning in this subject area relate to other subject areas?
- ◆ Are there similarities or connections in content, or in how it is being taught/learnt (pedagogy)?
- ◆ Are there similarities across subject areas in the skills being learnt?
- ◆ How will this help you in the future? Turn the discussion towards the students to determine how/if what is being taught will have relevance. The answer is that every 'soft skill' can be taught via any content area, so the skills of problem solving, collaboration, and creativity may come out via the process rather than via the content being learned.

Questions for your students to ask themselves

- ◆ What skills and content do you think will have the greatest need in the future?
- ◆ How does what we are learning relate back to you and your context?
- ◆ What do want to learn (content/skills) that has relevance to you and your context?
- ◆ How can you enhance or further develop your 'soft skills' outside of school?

◆ Are there times when you are practicing these skills that are harder/easier (e.g., home, friends, sports)? What makes it harder/easier and what can you learn from those experiences?

Notes

1   Saint-Exupéry, A. & Woods, K., *The Little Prince*, 1943. Print.
2   *Wizard of Oz*, Ibid.

A Flipped Solar System

Systems

♦ Why do we have an education system and what do we want our children to gain from it?
♦ Why do we have an education system and what do we want our society to gain from it?
♦ Who are we becoming?

Teaching and learning

♦ Why am I teaching this?
♦ What do I want my students to gain from it?
♦ Who are they becoming?

Learner

♦ Why is this so?
♦ Why does/doesn't this make sense/work?
♦ Who am I becoming?

DOI: 10.4324/9781003228066-13